LIFE'S TOO SHORT *for*
CHEAP CLING FILM

by

Maren Peters

Grosvenor House
Publishing Limited

This book is published by
Grosvenor House Publishing Ltd
28-30 High Street, Guildford, Surrey, GU1 3HY.
www.grosvenorhousepublishing.co.uk

This book is written as a source of information only.
The information and suggestions in this book should by no
means be considered a substitute for the advice of a qualified
medical professional if the need for medical attention arises.

A CIP record for this book
is available from the British Library

ISBN 978-1-907652-65-3

In loving memory of Mum

(1925 – 1975)

Maren Peters, born sometime in the 1960s, is a psychologist and until recently ran her own very busy life coaching practice. After many years of helping and encouraging countless women to find the true self in their lives, she decided it was time to share her discoveries of how to live an emotionally independent and untouchable life, a life immune to outside pressures and absurd influences, such as, for instance, weird diet systems or inappropriate men, or worse, still – both.

Maren is now a full-time writer and lives with husband Thomas, a chartered engineer, and a few wild cats in a little village in Buckinghamshire. Coming from a large family with very traditional values, she successfully managed to escape the traditional obligation of female family members to reproduce.

The two are living in a relationship of great individuality. The outcome – emancipation, surprisingly.

Note from the Author

I would like to thank all the wonderful women who over the years have shared their moving journeys discovering an independent life full of potential and contentment with me.

Every step of your way was as exhilarating and invigorating to me as it was to you.

Thank you.

Maren Peters

Acknowledgement

I would like to express a very special and very big thank you to my husband **Thomas**, who has supported me and my idea of finally putting this little book of freedom together and who so willingly stood by me while I was concentrating on this exciting adventure.

My living in front of a laptop and therefore rather obsessive behaviour for the past several months had me worried might have left him traumatised. He assures me he's fine.

Thomas, your endless supply of cups of iced tea, mineral water and cola drinks has played a very important role in all of this, as all your understanding and unconditional assistance has.

Your support fuelled me – *thank you.*

Contents

Foreword

This book is written for women. Obviously.

Old or young, tall or short, big and round or small
and tiny, skinny with chicken legs, curvy with one
bottom or with two, with big breasts, small breasts or
no breasts, with hair any style and colour or even with
no hair at all, with four children and no man or with
four men and no children, of all possible backgrounds
and with all possible futures – over the years I have
met hundreds of superb women and working with
them I have always found to be a great privilege.

While working with these beautiful personalities,
a few focal points of common interests and worries,
subjects of confusion and the overall desire to handle
certain situations and circumstances better have
crystallised; ten big ones, to be exact, and after several
years of collecting an enormous amount of affecting
information and visions, scares and cries for help,
solution-findings and new happiness, I felt inspired
to summarise these most desired liberations of today's
women – and how to achieve them – in this handy
book of great female freedom.

Especially the subject of personal freedom, to live a
fulfilled life without wasting any valuable time fighting
with cheap cling film or other nuisances like diets and
various men I have found to be of great trepidation to

all women. In a world close to crossing the line to insanity, women never felt more the need to be in control of their own lives; wishing to be independent and having a strong confidence to tackle obstacles of any nature is very much a fundamental desire within all of us. How to get there is another concern.

The experience all women I have worked with sooner or later shared was the discovery of frustrating emotional cages of various types, inevitably leading way too often into limiting and unhealthy compromises. Unhealthy as opposed to healthy compromises usually correlate to settling into situations or circumstances bearing one's limit or suppression rather than meeting in a healthy middle where both parties find give and take to be beneficial. Once this fine line vanishes, unhealthy restrictions usually creep in, overpowering any possibly useful compromise. Extracting whether the women had exposed themselves to these traps or others were to blame for the nature of their anxieties turned into an unearthing and satisfying journey of finding sovereignty.

Ludicrous affairs with men full of duplicity; sexual issues and curiosities; pointless or hopeless relationships; men's ex's and their seemingly grating influences; diets, diets and more diets; an unkind or even devastating childhood; a fairly bothersome family; the everlasting nervousness of ageing; being single or feeling stuck in a homemade comfort zone – pair these topics with feelings of vulnerability, worthlessness and suspicions of being a laughing stock, sprinkle a lack of self-esteem and self-confidence along with some good old-fashioned frustration on top of it and we have the perfect picture of gloom – welcome to the modern face of living.

The harmful and influential *depth* this modern face of our day-to-day life has on us remains greatly unnoticed. We might suspect certain room for improvement on a superficial level; the vicious reality of an emotional cage building up around us and within our subconscious, however, too often fails to transpire. It's worrying just how we habitually fall into patterns of exposure to constant outside pressures, while neglecting or suppressing our real wishes and slowly but surely sinking into deeper enslavement, invisible to the naked eye, but very noticeable to our hearts and to our at times hiding souls.

The resolution to breaking free from cages and limitations is to be found in a few very powerful words – **inner independence** towards whoever or whatever might cross our paths, a healthy **immunity** to the mayhem of the world around us and determined **untouchability.** These three words are key to receiving your well earned **self-confidence;** self-confidence resilient and vigorous enough to carry you from strength to strength with **self-acceptance** to be the ultimate outcome.

This book will take great pleasure in aiding you to release courage and curiosity, a touch of healthy selfishness, and finally facilitate a long overdue rescue of great magnitude.

'Life's too short for cheap cling film.'

Women United

Introduction

Have you ever fought – and lost – the battle with cheap cling film? The very low cost versions do come with a Health & Safety warning, however, the optimism to save a penny or two drives many to experiment with this bundle of annoyance. Although very good for the wallet, they're after all not first-rate on kitchen efficiency, sensitive female hands and female egos. The plastic film itself often is too thin and lacks adhesiveness, the cutting edge, in manufacturers' attempts to economise even further, is either too smooth, leaving you with a big knob of plastic in one hand, or too sharp, resulting in serious finger injury on the other hand. In desperation to cover leftover food, another confrontation fuelled with brave intentions to harvest some harmless cling film is faced, just to slice another finger.

It's frustrating, to say the least.

As far as could be established with any certainty, latest now the moment of truth has arrived. Getting the trainers out, throwing the whole packet of cling film onto the kitchen floor and jumping onto it is the next, however compulsive but logical deed. Two pretty severe finger injuries have so far not stopped anyone I know aiming to prove deserved justice. While jumping up and down in effort to destroy the evidence of poor economic appraisal, you promise yourself never to use cheap cling film again. The scars on two fingers will act as permanent reminders. Life's simply too short for this kind of trouble.

And yet life itself feels identical to battling with cheap cling film from time to time. We discover ourselves in situations tempted to jump onto; circumstances we desperately try to escape from or conditions we dread more than the arrival of bank statements, even if they showed some massive overdrafts. Unhealthy compromises seem to surround us, grabbing us against our will, and limit us at times beyond our control. When life feels like cheap cling film, we certainly wonder sometimes how we managed to end up in such a mess. The *depth* of this mess, however, and its impacts are often overlooked. Despite awareness of numerous annoying parts in day-to-day life, the extent to which we are being sucked into certain ways, certain habits and certain scenarios frequently goes unnoticed.

For many years I have collected real life stories, stories filled with emotions like anger and sadness, tears and laughter, illumination and liberation, tons of despair and masses of disappointed hopes, and they're simply too valuable to linger unshared – so here it is, the little book of the ten most principal and most sought after liberties I came across while working with many truly amazing female personalities. It also exemplifies a great unity, deeply welcomed by countless women and a harmony only us girls can truly relish, and it's such a shame I cannot introduce every individual woman's story outlining her constructive revolution delivering auxiliary motivation and evidence. Too many pages would be filled, but of both the support and solidarity of fellow women in similar situations you can be assured of.

The ten topics are in no particular order; some women find themselves in only one of the topics, some in more than one; this varies greatly. At any one time the reader can look up individual subjects; the chapters are not connected as such. What they do have in common, however, has ultimately something to do with inner independence, self-acceptance, self-esteem, self-confidence, untouchability and immunity or, in fact, *the lack of it.* By eliminating the lack of these powerful tools – and they truly are powerful – and by spicing up your personality to a degree always desired, your life can take a U-turn you wouldn't think was possible.

Some say the advice given in this little book might cause controversy; some say a number of suggestions on how to experiment with different approaches to various featured topics could even be considered highly unorthodox or at times too easy to be effective. Some find my proposals outraging. I have agreed to disagree with a few fellow psychologists on this; ruthlessly honest recommendations on occasion have proven to be out of the ordinary, yet surprisingly often also the most valuable. I leave it to you, the reader, to judge for yourself.

Since life's short, let's get straight to the point –
what would you like to free yourself from, what
would you like to discover, what are you tempted
to change? *Which embracing harmful compromise would
you like to escape from?*

Perhaps you are a woman who's on one side of an
affair with an otherwise so-called committed male,
and the enchanting fairy tale is slowly but surely
turning into a nightmarish reality, filled with infinite
hope, sad despair, endless ogling of the mobile phone
and the ever present question whether he'll leave
'her' or not? Women the world over find themselves
trapped in this one-way-system; if your life as the
affair hasn't began to suffer yet, it soon will. Meet
Jennifer and Emily in 'Affairs – a quick guide to
waking up to reality', as life – and diaries – tells the
best stories, and learn why men typically don't leave
their wives.

The pressures of a sex life that seems to have stopped
going anywhere, even though the arts of faking and
keeping up appearances have been mastered over the
years? 'Faker' or 'avoider' – which are you? Contrary to
a widely assumed bleakness, there's a clever solution to
be discovered. Take a chance and ascertain deliverance
of a formerly unknown prosperity in 'Sex – the sticky
subject'.

Diets, diets, *of course* – diets. Can you still count how
many times you have sampled the latest diet system,
be it group meetings, books, online advice or your
stick-insect cousin's guideline to convert to sushi?

How many times have you failed? A dozen times? Fifty times? Millions can validate that any diet advice sooner or later reveals to be not much more than yet a further bad experience to be added to the depressingly fat diary of failed diets. Welcome to the club of frustration, anger and resentment! To free oneself from the pressure of diets altogether, their ridiculous promises and the judgement of others on acceptable or unacceptable dress sizes is so close to women's hearts, they must be tattooed, reading 'Diets suck!'. Find out how to shed the worries over a few pounds too many, and celebrate being a woman – let's ditch diets ineradicably with the aid of the short 'Diets' chapter – *presumably the shortest piece about diets ever written!*

The partner's ex is another nuisance countless women clash with. Many relationships struggle due to what seems her never ending influence on life and harmony. When children are involved it's assumed one needs to work on growing a very thick skin as a first step. The sooner you start, you'll hear, the more prepared you'd become. It's thought to be crucial to re-evaluate and regroup your inner strength. Growing immunity proves even more sufficient than just increasing skin depth – or does it? The brief chapter 'The ex – factor' delivers a few embarrassingly simple tips and tricks for a previously unknown mutual and new understanding between the 'new' woman and the 'ex' woman; a combination widely assumed to be hopelessly competitive.

Are you a single lady and almost everybody around you expresses pity because you are considered a leftover of today's society and you wish they'd stop? Have you noticed just how many co-humans out there claim to know you better than you do and therefore feel free to criticise or give unasked advice whenever they like? Meet Rachel in 'Being single – bad luck or great privilege?'; not even all the Queen's donkeys and all the Queen's ladies could ever move her philosophy on this matter. The singleton within her rules for several good reasons, and sharing her revelation uplifted many single women.

Insecurities of several diverse natures hold women back everywhere. To huddle up in a self-made comfort zone seems reassuring only at first; do you assume you're trapped and does life somewhat feel bleak? With every passing day bathing in avoidance to stand up against yourself the dilemma will worsen. Comfort zones are very influential enemies, but with a spot on battle plan they can be contested. In 'Your comfort zone – how trapped are you?' you'll learn how, and Irene's encounters with herself will assist you on your way.

Family – do you describe yourself as somewhat unlucky on this battle front? Would you like to break free from the off-putting obligation to please certain family members? You're *not* alone. The number of women I have worked with experiencing a regular, almost uncontrollable urge to crush various heads easily exceeds the one hundred mark. Imagine your 'family' is a flock of sheep – and find out how to survive both, the wolves *and* the abattoir a little later in this book.

Being in that toxic relationship with an irritating male individual whose morning bathroom routine might include counting aloud the seconds spent spraying deodorant under his arm pits? Living with a man who's more committed to the remote control in his hand than any other device on the planet? It might sound weird, but there's not actually any 'wrong' or 'right' about a man; however, *there is the point of either fitting or, more often, not fitting.* Find out how the knowledge and wisdom of 'compatibility' will either make or break a relationship. Countless women already feel like skipping the entire relationship business for once and for all, as too many unhealthy compromises caused their inner self to, what some explain, retract to be a shadow of the former self. The chapter 'Relationships and Men – necessity or just 'funny things?" introduces a few tips and tricks.

All these topics, but also experiences stemming from a childhood long gone and their potentially good influences for adulthood you'll find covered in this book. In 'Childhood – the most pleasant time of your life?' you'll have a brief insight to an autobiographic example. Whichever topic might be appealing, the aim is to arm any woman seeking personal freedom and shedding emotional cages and restraining compromises with the insight required to travel this rather captivating journey of self-discovery.

Self-acceptance – particularly when it comes to ageing – is the most powerful tool in the female world, and it's truly worth discovering. Vanity typically obtains a punch gazing into the mirror rather unexpectedly –

the face is beginning to succumb to gravity, a few pounds too many hold on ruthlessly, grey hair appears miraculously overnight as early as in the twenties, age spots appear in the late thirties, the eyesight is weakening by the time one hits forty – this *can* all be dealt with, even quite easily. A healthy curiosity and relaxed attitude, a good sense of humour and the gift to not take oneself too seriously work wonders when facing bodily decay.

The same applies to one's thoughts and emotions. Before anyone can *live* how they feel, it's required to accept that those believes and feelings are as much a necessity as frequently purchasing handbags. To therefore enjoy their own decisions is a special freedom countless women seek. But self-acceptance is not limited to the appearance, thoughts or inclinations of a person; more so some actions and behaviours also deserve to simply be accepted for what they are – a part of you, a component that makes a human in its entirety a unique being. If you are a smoker, you'll find this is probably the only guide / personal development book to suggest *not* giving up smoking. I do not smoke myself, but I appreciate that many people do. To self-accept that smoking, for the time being, is an element of 'you' is more sensible than losing the battle to quit on a loop of 30-minute intervals. Inevitably feeling like a failure will only lead to grabbing yet another cigarette. Be easy on yourself; accept that you're a smoker for now. When quitting feels better than continuing, you'll know. Until then, enjoy your smoke.

Quirks, especially entertaining ones, represent another beautifully individual way to discover self-acceptance.

If you find yourself living the habit of organising your fridge contents edging towards obsession or you can't but iron your knickers, followed by folding them into symmetrical triangles simply accept it – it's ok.

Self-acceptance doesn't resemble giving up or giving in. It's not about admitting defeat or finding the easiest way to avoid change, like so often being stuck in a comfort zone represents. It simply stands for accepting the terms and conditions of being human, of *not* being perfect. We all are individuals with different ideas and plans, dreams and emotions, challenges and experiences. The chapter dedicated to 'self-acceptance' at the end of this little book of freedom will deliver truly valuable insights to this most imperative of all tools.

To live a life as free as possible is the ultimate wish. We are all aware of this desire, the truth is, however, we don't always get there straight away; some of us might never do. Whether we are hindered by others or ourselves, the journey through life trying to minimise unhealthy compromise and to maximise uplifting happiness is never as easy as it ought to be, and it certainly requires a true and strong courage, a carrying self-confidence, and an independence of bigger measures.

The repetitive yet brief mention of inner independence, immunity, untouchability, self-confidence and self-acceptance is intended and you'll find throughout this book. These wonderful words are undeniably of vital importance; they are the hidden armada of secret weapons facilitating your inner self to lead a life exactly to your liking. Whichever topic in this book calls you – a strong inner independence, a healthy immunity and determined untouchability are key factors.

Self-confidence resulting from self-acceptance is after all what it comes down to – *the* keyword in countless women's lives and the source of all your powers. The tools to obtain this most central of all possible female vigour are very closely interconnected. You can't really have independence without self-confidence or be immune to an outside influence without being to a certain extent untouchable. However, once established, self-confidence will force any outside pressure to crumble down to nothing more than a minor irritation.

The characteristics of this discovery often cause women to become a little impatient. Once the decision is made to improve one's life, results are eagerly yearned for. To remain relaxed and calm, to allow focus to happen without pressure and to see the funny side if new outcomes take a little longer to show up is strongly advised. Be patient with yourself if what you uncover feels a little weird to begin with, foreign or even scary, because it will. However, the happy ending will be your personal freedom, filled with a new, stronger self-confidence, empowering you to live exactly as you please.

One weighty preface remains
We're almost at the point for you to commence your expedition. Before we proceed deeper into the jungle,

there's one more and most crucial advice to be taken onboard at this stage, advice of vital importance. It outlines your future path and will not only determine but dictate the way you'll experience the journey ahead. It's very simple, yet can be daunting, so bear with yourself - ***don't be afraid of your own conviction and bravery.*** A lot of women have never *truly* felt any powerful daring, what it *really* feels like, as for too long or too often their paths or visions were blocked and a very consuming daily emotional and habitual trot was common place. When you feel courage building up inside of you, don't shy away from it. Summon it and begin exploring. Courage always feels eerie at first, but if you allow it to grow it will sooner or later give you the precious self-confidence you seek, enabling you to establish immunity, untouchability and inner independence.

A little footnote
Having been in the advice-business for many years, one can't but notice the vast number of suggestion books and leaflets, CD's, DVD's and other programmes on the market and to what lengths some associate advisors go to fill pages and pages and more pages in their contributions to the well-being of fellow humans. At times, these initiations tend to be thinner than appreciated, despite filling tons of paper; my belief and therefore approach, however, is different. I don't consider advice books of any subject to fulfil their purposes too well if the advice offered is overloading with cyclic information flows, too enormous to be taken in efficiently and too overly complicated to convert 'advice' to 'action' with successful 'change' to be the desired effect.

Heartfelt advice doesn't have to be expensive, dense or lengthy to be valuable. The little book of freedom offers brief, accessible and explicable advice, without weighing heavily in one's handbag or cutting corners in its effectiveness. Some chapters are longer, some are shorter. Its main aspiration is to deliver an ally strong enough to assist women on their quests to a fulfilled 'inside', eventually converting this hidden beauty to be visibly admired on the 'outside', but being handy at the same time. Anybody feeling the need to criticise this approach, please feel free.

Let's go!
All this said and done – let's go, let's do it. Give yourself priority from now on and see for yourself what you've always suspected – life is indeed too short to fight with cheap cling film.

Have a great journey.

'It's not a Princess's life being involved
with a married man.
At first it might look like he's the King of the
Castle, going to make you his Queen, but when you
look closely you realise
he's just the dungeon's dragon.
Only less attractive.'

Emily

Affairs – a quick guide to waking up to reality

Unless one has self-harm tendencies or enjoys being an
affair in its pure nature without the need to incorporate
any plans for a harmonious future, hardly anything is
as nerve-wracking and emotionally daunting as being
involved with a spoken for man. Any woman who
has ever been in this 'arrangement' will confirm the
insanity of it. Over the years I have found the number
of women involved in affairs to be shockingly high; the
emotional minefield their positions trigger is immense,
and I haven't met one single lady concerned who
wasn't filled with the urgent desire to escape the
poignant roller coaster this situation sooner or later
unavoidably develops into. To have found many on
the brink of chopping either their lovers' or their own
heads off should come as no surprise.

This chapter wishes to attend to both parties of the
tragedy that affairs signify – the woman primarily
linked to the cheating man but predominantly the

woman being the man's affair. The most common form of affairs consists of women who are strictly speaking single and find themselves in a relationship with a married or otherwise committed man, with his sense of commitment to be questionable, of course. The following pages are meant as guidance for those who, once the novelty aspect of the affair has worn off, face a mountain of unfulfilled hopes, endless waiting and impairing despair. Every woman ever having been involved with a swindling man would also verify that more or less everything in the so-called relationship usually has to go according to his terms and conditions; the own ideas or beliefs often take a back seat – just one of many unpleasant side effects of being an 'affair'. What so often begins as a harmless flirt frequently turns into nightmares.

Although mainly to forewarn potential affairs for their own benefit, this chapter also addresses the trauma of the betrayed wife or partner. Unfortunately, very often the wife/partner doesn't immediately suspect any wrongdoing committed by the other half. A whole heap of suspicions usually has to build up before any proper clarification takes place. Once one eventually finds out, how to react is not automatically obvious to many. The shock hits hard, but the reality of this life altering impact hits even harder, as very often factors like wealth, children, social status and more might be at stake.

Affair or wife/partner – both sides have a variety of problems and challenges at hand, changing frequently. For the affair, filled with fears to be jammed into a relationship that is doomed to go nowhere, troubles change on a daily basis, beginning with waiting and hoping and ending in despair and disappointment. For the betrayed wife/partner after discovering the truth, a completely new bunch of problems presents itself. The consequences of such a discovery are indeed life changing. However, once accommodating the new circumstances and accepting that he's not worth any tears, the pleasure of chucking the cheating, annoying and idiotic subject can bare rather liberating and previously unknown satisfaction.

For now, this chapter wishes to focus on all those girls in the wild world of wishful thinking who might be toying with the idea of entering or already are in a shagging relationship – let's face it, despite the twaddle he might tell you about you being wonderfully different on every facet, that's usually what it is – and becoming part of a game which might look tempting at first, but usually over time will involve not only endless disappointments, more waiting and more hoping, but also unfulfilled all day day-dreaming of palm beaches, wedding cakes and Cinderella shoes. The reality of this game is certainly very different, as many women filled with heart-broken sadness would confirm.

The truth involves facing lonely and cold nights, staring psychotically at the mobile phone, especially at weekends, numerous unanswered queries and the desire to raid the fridge. One should be prepared for pure and naked confrontation with very alarming realism. In addition to these already depressing factors remains a worrying question to crumble over – 'Does he still do 'it' with her?', closely followed by 'Will he ever leave her for me?'.

Whether one is the affair or the wife/partner after finding out, both parties independently go through the notions of emotions beyond anybody's belief unless they have been in this painful game themselves. It's a thoroughly upsetting arrangement, and I have only met a handful of women who would do the affair side all over again, sadly. On a positive note, therefore *almost all* women concerned literally never touched a married or involved man again. After realising the dead-end of the matter, they were cured for once and for all. As far as the betrayed wives/partners are concerned, their overall vision of marriage had suffered a substantial hit and its institution faced a loss of trust on more than one level. All women I have worked with being forced into experiencing the upmost treachery have never married again and were handling future adventures involving men with chaste scepticism.

Being in the position of the outsider obtaining the position of the insider, it's illuminating to observe the persona change women on both sides acquire once the penny dropped, even if it took a whole pound to rattle down the mind. The yearning for independence is hardly ever shown on a greater scale.

It's now time to introduce an amazing true-life story, one that deeply impressed me; it's accurate what can be stumbled on in philosophical manifests, collected

by many wise people over the centuries – life still
writes the best stories.

I remember one particular account which became
more than just a curious case in my files; it became a
movie, perfectly fit for the big screen – a movie about
the betrayed wife and the awoken affair teaming up
and chucking the object of annoyance together…

One day I received a parcel delivered to my office
address. It had been posted anonymously, was quite
a big and heavy pack, and the postman seemed happy
to be getting rid of it. I didn't pay too much attention
at first, as it could have been all sorts of things. It
could have been just another marketing ploy where
manufacturers of whatever product you most likely
don't need try to catch your attention by sending
mysterious looking packages. It could have also been
my accountant's latest discovery of a book helping
me to organise my paperwork more efficiently,
seeking relief from mountains of formalities.

But it wasn't. The content of the parcel took part
in becoming one of my most remarkable cases.
The case of two women, strangers to one another,
finding a true and outright independence and
friendship to last. The affair and the wife. Two
women. One story.

In the parcel was a diary.

I randomly flicked through it, trying to make out
what this was all about. Quickly I found myself

intrigued, reading passages like 'I'm sure I must be more important to him by now' and 'will he ever leave her? She doesn't do it for him anymore, he said' or 'I can't believe he stood me up.'

The whole diary was overflowing with one story, which undoubtedly was the excruciating summary of a woman and a married man conducting their affair. I flicked through the book again. There was no letter or even just a note to me, nothing. Whoever had sent this parcel must have something in mind, I thought, still finding it peculiar to have received such an unusual correspondence. I looked for a note or message once more, a bit more thoroughly this time, but there was just this chunky book of what became clear by reading even only brief fragments was a book of big emotions, big hopes, big disappointments and at times self-explanatory anecdotes about the main character in this story – the selfish, self-centred, moral-free man. His name was Nathan. To serve authenticity, the wording of this account remains original.

September 1st, 09:37p.m.
Here I am, twenty-eight years of age, and I feel like a teenager. A girlie teenager! And what do girlie teenagers do? They keep diaries. So the first thing I did in my lunch break today was to buy this diary. I think I'll call you Maude.

Dear Maude,
Why I feel like a teenager again? Because I have the biggest crush on this guy and I'm bursting to talk

about it – but I can't. Not to a fellow human being anyway; those I know would neither approve nor understand. Why? Because he's married. And to make matters worse, with three children. Yes, I managed to lay my eyes on a married man. Of course Mother would say my whole world has been cocked up for most of my existence, so fantasising about a man with a ring on his wedding finger represented a completely normal disaster for me.

He's a colleague and to be honest, I don't really know how it all happened – it just did. I've always fancied him a little. He's older than me, thirteen years, really good looking, great hair and eyes to bathe in. I know I shouldn't even be thinking like this, him being married and all that, but I can't help myself. Last week something inside me made 'click' when we were in this meeting at work together and he dropped a pen while standing at the white board, presenting some numbers, bent down to pick up the pen which exposed his rather well formed derrière, and I've been looking at him with different eyes ever since.

His name is Nathan and I just love the way he pays attention to me. He's complementing my looks and my work, and flirts flirts flirts, all the time. He might be married, but I think it must be an unhappy relationship with his wife – would he otherwise look at me the way he does and flirt flirt flirt? Goosebumps and butterflies!

I took a breather after only the very first entry made by this woman whose name I didn't know. I heaved a sigh and shook my head. Goosebumps and butterflies –

completely normal when first directing all the energies of passion into a person, even if totally inappropriate. Apparently, he was irresistible; countless women the world over have fallen for mouth-watering male maligned advances disguised as compliments and shameful flirts, their normal senses failing. Sudden unexplainable blindness strikes and any obvious details surrounding the newly found love interest eclipse. Even *if* unhappily married, feeling stuck in a dying relationship and dreaming of a new life, being married with children remains naked fact, a reality which never supports an apt starting point for any new liaison. I continued reading; the next entry came as no surprise.

September 6th, 10:03p.m.

Dear Maude,

What an evening last night! And what a night! We all went out for a drink after completing this big deal we all have been working on like idiots for weeks, and I couldn't help but enjoy a few drinks too many. I didn't fall into a coma, but became pleasantly legless. Legless enough to hang around Nathan all night, returning his flirts – he was in good form.

What can I say – we did it…!!! After a few more drinks and when everybody was leaving Nathan asked me if he can buy me a night cap, and before I knew it we were in this lovely hotel located near the pub, with this gorgeous bar, lots of mirrors and oil paintings on the walls. He ordered a bottle of bubbly and parked me there, and ten minutes later he waved the plastic key to a hotel room in my face.

'I hope I've read your mood right, honey', he said. In hindsight, his look reminded me of a poodle's face, possibly on death row, truly hard to resist! We got on really well, talked about all sorts of irrelevant things and laughed a hell of a lot. The room number was 0911 – I trust it's not a bad omen, as I'm too happy to worry about such things.

We made love twice last night, before he had to leave to get home. I stayed in the hotel, after all the room was paid for. Strangely, I feel no remorse. I'm confused, yes, but weirdly happy. I bet this is how a Princess must feel – hotel, taxi back home this morning, bubbly at the bar. Have I found the Prince??? Has my time to find somebody special finally come??? Oh, I hope so…! Goosebumps and butterflies!

I can't but wonder… he was so enthusiastic… when did he last do 'it'? It's none of my business, I guess. Anyway, I'm smiling; I could dance around in joy. But my hangover disagrees with such straining activity.

I quickly browsed over the days and weeks to follow this event, but then decided to read the diary front to back, page by page, not peeking at the last bits, and it was rather unmistakable – the two had began a full blown affair, with faux business trips on Nathan's side, with further organised hotel stays every Tuesday and Thursday, with passionate sex games involving sex toys and pornographic movies, with naughty text messaging during the days and sometimes at weekends and with a secret sign language between them whenever they had to share a business at work. Sometimes she was preparing meals for him, mostly they went out. Whatever costs occurred, he paid happily.

During the first weeks everything seemed to go well for this mysterious woman who'd sent me her diary. They even had planned a mini-break away, to take place just before Christmas. Her entries to this book of passion, how she called the diary apart from 'Maude', reflected happiness, and her excitement towards Nathan became obvious; spending as much time with him as possible became priority, and she made herself available whenever he had any amount of time for her, even if it was only for a quick coffee at a motorway service station. Neither walking nor waiting in pouring rain to get a quick glimpse of him would stop her. Get-togethers with friends or family were cancelled at short notice, if he'd unexpectedly become available; she'd do anything to accommodate his schedules. His part in all of this was simple – he made her feel special. Every bit of attention he paid her was savoured. The time they had together, she made sure was special for him, too, so special in fact, she hoped he wanted to stay forever. Then, one day, the Princess's fairy tale started to tremor…

November 30th, 08:41 p.m.
Dear Maude,
I can't believe I'm sitting here in this restaurant, waiting and waiting and waiting. Nathan had texted and said he's going to be a little late, but I've been waiting for more than two hours by now and haven't heard anything further from him! The staff in this place keep looking at

me; I suspect they think I'm a prostitute. Not a surprise, really, since I'm wearing this rather skimpy outfit. In order to not look quite so pathetic waiting on my own, I thought it's best to keep busy, hence my writing this now.

I don't really know what to make of this – this is strange; it has never happened before! Wanna know what else I find strange? I tell you – it's the rather unexpected phone conversation we had late last night; he managed to sneak out of the house, said it couldn't wait until today to inform me that our normal Tuesday and Thursday arrangement can't continue and that it won't do so until further notice.

'Something's not right, you know, Jennifer might suspect something and I don't want to risk the fun times you and I have together' – he said. I wanted to ask if something had happened, but he cut me off, adding 'I've got too much on before Christmas, honey, gotta cancel our trip, too. Will make it up to you, I promise. Gotta go. Bye.' He had put the phone down without even waiting for a reply. Was it raining last night and he needed to get back into the house? I can't recall.

I can't believe he's standing me up… only last night he said we have fun times! I miss him. Maybe he can free some other time soon. I could cook him that Moroccan tagine again, only this time without tarragon, as it, very unfortunately for the little IKEA rug on my kitchen floor, had made him vomit violently last time.

According to the final entry of the day, Nathan had eventually texted her to at long last cancel their planned dinner, without further explanation. After a couple more drinks at the bar, the restaurant staff had relocated her to a place where she wouldn't occupy a whole table without even eating anything, and when she about a further hour later took a taxi home, it was the first time since she had started seeing Nathan that an incredible loneliness fell over her. To compensate this, she tried to excuse his behaviour, tried to convince her brain of the lack of real influence he had on planning his evenings, tried to persuade her bruised soul that the job of resilience to prove sympathy and adaptability was upon her. After all, he did have a wife and three children, two girls and a boy, and they needed him, as the kids were still young, sixteen, ten and four years of age. This factual element she intuitively understood; at some point she had written a long paragraph about her feelings towards his children, and how she hoped they'd be fine if he ever contemplated leaving his family for her. Secretly, she was rehearsing what to say to them the first time they might meet, one day.

She went to bed nightmaring about a long weekend spent away, together with his wife and children and lots of cuddly toys, and even his mother-in-law, wrapped into an apron reading 'Mothers know best' appeared in her dream; a grumpy, old and faceless woman who could have also been her own mother. A poodle kept re-appearing, so did mountains of white cabbage with silly faces, and she woke up in a cold sweat only an hour after going to bed.

Although it was in the middle of the night and totally against some rules introduced at the beginning of their affair, she couldn't resist – she had to dial his mobile phone number, ensuring her caller ID would not be displayed, obeying at least this rule.

Never before had she broken the 'never-call-or-text-me-when-I'm-probably-at-home' rule, but she found a million justifications to dial his number anyway. The alcohol still circulating in her bloodstream didn't support any rational decision making process at this point. What happened next robbed yesterday's cancellation of the Tuesday / Thursday arrangement of any relevant significance.

Jennifer, his wife, picked up, sounding rather out of breath. With that typical too far a distance between mouth piece and already talking Mystery Woman heard her say '… oh, yes, it was amazing, Nath, and I want you at least once more tonight.' Then a little louder, the mouth now properly aligned with the mobile phone: 'Hello? Nathan Strang's phone. Jennifer speaking.'

December 5th, 11:45p.m.
Dear Maude,
We went out for dinner 'afterwards', as Nathan didn't fancy the idea of a tagine at home.

I wish I had more guts… All this stuff… I never thought it would cross my mind to perhaps bother me; I guess I've always assumed things were wonky between Nathan and his wife. Otherwise, why…?

Shall I ask him – shall I ask 'the' question?

He behaved as always; no sign of him having any extra worries or suspecting me behind that phone call late the other night, but he anyway never really speaks his mind. All evening I pretended all is fine, didn't even ask about our cancelled trip or T & T arrangements. Not a word from him, either.

I feel like having learnt about a dirty secret or even having accidentally witnessed a committed crime and now not being sure what to really do with this information. Police or blackmail spring to mind. Neither would really work in my case, as the police wouldn't give a damn about my emotions and blackmailing only works if one actually has some proof of a person's action to be wrong. Having sex with one's wife unfortunately isn't illegal.

How often do they do it – birthdays, anniversaries, Bank Holidays, Christmas, Easter and American Independence Day? Or do I have to add christenings, weddings and pub quiz nights to this list???

The question began to eat Mystery Woman; and although a self-declared coward, the urge for an answer was greater than the impulse to avoid the subject.

December 6th, 11:22p.m.
Dear Maude,
I summoned all my courage and asked him. My guesswork had kept me awake all night and I simply

needed to know. When he had a minute, we met in a conference room this morning, pretending to go through some work stuff together.

The news was expected, yet excruciating. Of course I had blushed like a lobster boiling unhappily away in water when I enquired 'we never really talked about it, but do you still have sex with your wife?'. I had crossed my fingers on one hand under the table, hoping for a miracle despite the pressing facts.

'Lately…, well, you know', he began quite humbly, almost shy, and avoiding any eye contact. This little boy behaviour was completely new to me. Nathan usually represented a standing man in his prime. Now, his face was poodle-like again. I said nothing.

'I *have* to sleep with her! You must understand, if I didn't she'd be suspicious; she's already behaving strangely.' Then he added 'I don't want to fib you, honey.'

I somewhat had the feeling he expected praise.

I just looked at him, no, I stared at him, not saying a word. Suddenly, his humble shyness was gone. I was still looking for words, but I couldn't think of anything appropriate to reply. 'C'mon, honey', don't spoil your day', he changed the subject, 'Here, I have a surprise for you. Came in only this morning.'

He handed me an envelope.

Early January they went on a long weekend trip together. Paris, City of Love. Leaving London on the

Eurostar, first class, and a five star hotel awaiting them at the other end; everything was heavenly. The pages of the diary covering this time are full of laughter, fun, and lots of sex, wine, croissants and music. Any of Mystery Woman's worries were blown away by the experience of feeling like a million dollars. Nathan successfully convinced her to lose any anxiety regarding his sex life with his wife, encouraged her to not agonise about such irrelevant facts; nothing, he said, was important, but their time together. One evening, after a long walk along the Seine River, he charitably promised to take her away for her birthday in a few months.

He was funny, kind and attentive, spoiled her when attacking the shops on the Champs Elysees, spoiled her in the evenings with illustrious dinners and spoiled himself at night when they had sex until they were physically too exhausted to continue. Then, when slouching in bed together, he whispered sweet little nothings into her ears; not exactly any 'I love you's' but words pleasing enough to fuel her hopes for a true commitment from his side, perhaps one day, perhaps soon. In those moments she felt what she would call 'love' for him. Her emotions when holding him close were positively more than just a crush.

Her pressing loneliness and the evident disappointments, the waiting and hoping and the horror about him still doing 'it' with his wife back in the real world was forgotten as if nothing had ever happened. What he might have told his wife regarding his whereabouts for a long weekend she didn't know about and she didn't seem to have asked. If she had, she must have chosen to not waste any thoughts, ink or pages on this subject, as her diary revealed nothing. Most likely she had disconnected from the fact that her lover was married.

Their wonderful time together made her wish ever more for a united life. Summarising their trip and other good spells in the past fuelled her beyond pragmatism. A new question was burning deep inside her; slowly but surely it became stronger, and it was only a matter of sufficient red wine intake until it would emerge. She *needed* to know, in fact, it felt outright legitimate in her mind. Although he had never shown *real* signs to support any similar intensions, she made a mental note to address him as soon as an opportunity would arise. One evening, in a very romantic little restaurant near the hotel and with stunning views of the Eiffel Tower, when they were nibbling strange looking complimentary little creatures the waiter had assured them were edible, she summoned all her courage once more and asked him the fragile question, filled with new hope – 'Do you think our lives will ever be different from what they are now, yours and mine, I mean, you know, in terms of a joint future?'

Nathan's reply equalled a slap involving rotten fish across her face; it was the first and last nail in her coffin. 'What should change, honey, isn't it good just the way it is? Besides, I've never said I wanted any sort of a joint future, or how you call it, have I? I don't need another wife, I have one.'

A French waiter, contrary to the usual fashion of ignoring paying customers, looked truly concerned when he saw the blood leaving her face. Making an effort, in broken English he asked if there was something the matter with the food, insisting once more on its edibility.

The man sitting opposite her became a stranger. Slowly, the memories from even just a few hours earlier disappeared in a peculiar cloud. She tried to read his face but couldn't find him in there. 'What?', he asked, startled, oddly openly revealing his usually hidden thoughts, gazing at her crossly. 'You're not really surprised, are you, honey? C'mon, don't spoil it; here, have some more wine.' He filled her glass.

After a short while of sitting silently and witnessing Nathan fighting with French delicatessen her head began to throb as if been hit with something big and heavy; wearily, she stood up, grabbed her coat and her bag, and walked off. Her legs felt stiff, but she managed to proceed to the exit. Reaching it felt like hours going by, yet it only took seconds. When leaving through the revolting restaurant door she heard him yell 'Hey! Where the hell you think you're going? You can't just leave me here! I can't eat all this shit on my own!'

Strangely, she felt no pity for him.

Valentine's Day, 08:56p.m.
Dear Maude,
I'm celebrating my stupidity. The emptiness I felt at first was not just surreal, it was paralysing. I haven't been

taking notes for some weeks, as you know – but today
I thought it's appropriate to have a drink and to write
down a thing or two.

Drinking rum doesn't really help, but I'm drinking
anyway. It might take away the humiliation and
embarrassment, if only for a moment or so. At least
I have you, dearest Maude. Shame you can't join me
for a drink.

Jennifer could though…

Pages after pages pouring out her sorrow followed.
She had dreamed about and longed for making a
difference to this man's life, and to her own life, too.
But it was never going to happen. Her hopes had
failed her spectacularly.

Rather unexpectedly, a warm and honest concern for
Jennifer and the children and all the pain she might
have caused found a way into the diary. None the
wiser at first, suddenly, while reading these angry,
disappointed and drunken lines, only a few pages
away from the finale, something in my head fell into
place. I couldn't believe I had missed it! I looked up
some notes I usually keep of my clients. Here it was –
Jennifer Strang.

Jennifer had been my client for quite some time.
I hadn't seen her for a couple of weeks by then. My
notes refreshed my memory; she hadn't actually come

to see me for a specific reason at first, had just wanted
a good old chat, which happens from time to time.
A bit of a natter can work wonders.

She was a very good looking woman to anybody's
taste, was in her early forties, mature and elegant,
seemed in control and content. These first impressions
never remain in their lines for long though, and within
minutes the true nature of one's troubles usually
breaks through. Jennifer was not just suspecting her
husband had an affair, she was certain of it – all the
evidences she had collected wouldn't allow any other
suggestion. He had always worked hard, but one day,
out of the blue, his workload appeared to have tripled,
and he stayed away overnight frequently. Amazingly,
some additional overnight stays regularly occurred on
Tuesdays and Thursdays and lasted for several weeks.
I recalled her wondering, with a pale smile, how
stupid he thought she might be.

What proved her point undoubtedly was his overall
changed behaviour towards her. Long lost romantic
gestures seemed revived, and her mobile phone kept
overflowing with text messages telling her how
beautiful and special she was. A suggested mini-
break, just before Christmas and without the children,
caused Jennifer's eyebrows not just to raise but to
arch. 'It's probably his way of trying to not sow
unnecessary seeds of suspicion,' Jennifer said,
'which is ironic, as that's exactly what he did.'

The nature of the real bomb that blew her
comprehensible proof of Nathan's affair into her

face genuinely surprised her. 'He started to show an innovative interest in me, sexually, I mean. I tell you, that came as a true shock to me, as our sex life had been limited to doing it once at Christmas and once on May Bank Holiday. It had been like this since our youngest was born, so for some years now. He clearly must think I'm stupid. I suppose it's true what they say; guilty people do make the first move.'

Jennifer had found out about her husband's affair within weeks; his attempts to compensate for his unfaithful activities outside the wedlock were too obvious to miss.

Still wondering why this diary had found its way to me, I thought of the only logical reason; instinctively, although I hadn't intended to peek, I flicked to the very last page of the diary.

February 20th, 09:34p.m.
Dear Maude,
I went to Nathan's house today... I couldn't sit still in my lunch break, so I got into my car and off I went. Nathan's been ignoring me as if we were complete strangers ever since I had fled from Paris on the next plane out. I still praise the fact I usually carry my passport and emergency money around with me at all times! When on an escape it surely comes in handy.

There's so much traffic going on in my brain – I expect my dull grey cells to eventually end up in a massive collision, destroying each other. For almost a week now

I find I have only one thought emerging from the mess in my head - I need to tell Jennifer. I need to confess to her what I've done and more importantly I want her to know what an arsehole she's married to.

But I couldn't do it. No courage as usual... I just sat there in my car, a couple of houses away from their drive, unable to move. My brain was frying along, I wanted to move, but my body just wouldn't. Then I saw her.

Jennifer was leaving the house. She was even more beautiful than I remembered from that family photograph on the sideboard in Nathan's office. Why on earth would he cheat on her? She certainly looks lots more to look at than me...

Jennifer was getting into a car, driving off. I don't know what possessed me, but I followed her. After about ten minutes she parked up, left her car and walked towards what looked like an office building. I awkwardly parked at a discrete distance, trying to avoid being seen.

When she arrived at the office building I saw her push a huge door bell with a name next to it on a letter box. She got buzzed in and I took a deep breath. As if operated by remote control, I got out of my car and went to have a look. The sign next to the door bell read: Maren Peters, TheLifeCoach.

All of a sudden everything became blindingly obvious, and I understood why I was holding this diary in my hands. Mystery Woman wanted Jennifer to find out about her affair with Nathan, her conscience plagued her, yet she simply couldn't face a possibly negative confrontation, couldn't bring herself to tell Jennifer directly. Unaware that Jennifer already knew, very cleverly she'd put one and one together, took a wild shot and hoped the betrayed wife would receive access to 'Maude the diary' this way; and she did.

During the next appointment I presented the 'memoirs of an affair' to Jennifer. Our sessions so far had evolved around her life with Nathan and their three children, and although she was sure about his clandestine affair, taking her time exploring her own feelings towards him before making a decision about his infidelity was central to her. She admitted she liked seeing him suffer, letting him believe all is well and enjoyed the theatre performance he staged for her when trying his latest seduction techniques.

I explained how this book came to be in my possession and mentioned a few passages I had read about Mystery Woman's struggle with bravery; I also very carefully confirmed that the suspicions of her husband's furtiveness were indeed accurate. Everything Jennifer had referred to in our meetings, all of Nathan's whereabouts and out of the ordinary activities were precise. Whatever else Jennifer hadn't established yet, the diary would hold answers to it all.

I had thought about it long and hard and I came to the conclusion that only the confrontation with this book would count as frank help here. Once adequately strong, I was convinced Mystery Woman would try and find other ways of contacting Jennifer, in case her attempt via the sessions with my client, the betrayed wife, was to fail.

I had asked Jennifer upfront whether or not she wanted to sustain confrontation with so many details about her husband's affair; I warned her about certain sordid information to be found in this book. Jennifer collected her thoughts for a few seconds, and then reached out. When I handed her the diary, she cried, having a tight grip with both hands around it. Her tears only lasted a brief moment. She flicked through the diary just as I had done when I first received it, and her facial expression was changing. The moan disappeared without trace, and I noticed a new determination and enlightenment in her eyes. She read aloud a few words she found by chance, summarising Mystery Woman's concern for the children. Jennifer didn't pussyfoot around the subject, and with what seemed a great concern for a total stranger she said 'I want to meet her, no, in fact, I *need* to meet her; and after what you've suggested regarding her lack of courage, I'm sure she's hoping for my move to be the next. And I don't intend to disappoint her. Can we do it here? This sofa seems cosy enough for such an important encounter.'

One week later they met in my office. Jennifer had come across no obstacle tracking the unknown woman down; her name was Emily. Nathan still had her number in his mobile phone. Under 'H' for 'Honey' Jennifer had found what she was seeking. Men…

The positive absence of even the slightest peculiarity between the two women was extraordinary. Jennifer had arrived first, and while waiting for Emily, she seemed calm, but very keen to get this endeavour on the way. She gave the impression to be more resolute than ever, and I remember checking out the size of Jennifer's handbag; secretly I feared she might have a sledge hammer or some other sort of weapon hidden in her bag, and I really didn't like the idea of a bloody fight or any other wrestle taking place in my office.

Nothing even remotely close happened – when Emily arrived the two women briefly gazed at each other, and then, to my utter surprise, Jennifer jumped up from the sofa, and as I already feared for the worst, she opened her arms wide and Jennifer and Emily hugged like long lost friends. Tears followed, but luckily I was armed with lots of tissue boxes all over my office.

They talked for hours. Jennifer had brought the diary, and they went through it in sync, almost page by page. Nothing they read seemed to have any negative effect on Jennifer. Certain details and descriptions of sexual practices Jennifer took in and referred to as if they were weather reports. Emily, who looked utterly ashamed for their entire congregation, completely devout and modest, seemed grateful for Jennifer's tranquillity. I had seen it in many women before – despite painful grief, the mind starts to repair itself lots sooner than many imagine. Starting in the subconscious, it quickly progresses from there.

To see these two women sitting close together and watching them share snotty bits of tissue re-assured me that miracles *do* happen. Witnessing this felt like a new dimension of friendship pretty much unknown to mankind had just been born.

When the evening drew to an end both women were free of tears. Emily must have emphasised her remorse about the affair with Jennifer's husband at least a hundred times, vividly avoiding the word 'husband' and referring to Nathan as 'the bastard', and how grateful she was to have met Jennifer, a fact almost jeopardised by her lack of courage

'He's such an unbelievable misfit', Jennifer said, 'he made both of us look like fools. But we're no idiots, and I believe we should demonstrate that. By the way, do you have any further plans tonight?' Jennifer now spoke with disgust in her voice, leaping up from the sofa, pulling an unsuspecting Emily along. 'No, I don't, and I think I know why you're asking', Emily replied, re-adjusting the lopsided sleeves of her blouse after Jennifer's energetic outburst.

A day later, all was said and done. Jennifer and Emily had gone to the soon to be former matrimonial home of Jennifer's and had confronted Nathan on the spot. He had been at home, babysitting the children, and I don't think they broke the news gently. I learnt he had looked rather shocked at first, regretful a bit later and had been pathetically begging in his last instance, but Jennifer had made very clear that their relationship ended there and then. Merciless, she gave him an hour to pack his things.

In Emily Jennifer had found a true friend, and it wasn't guilt or the desire to make up for any caused pain why Emily offered her comradeship. Emily herself learnt an enormous amount about inner independence, inner freedom, solidarity and true concern, self-confidence, courage and determination. The time the two women spent together was beneficial for both of them, and the fact that Emily developed a sister-like relationship with the children was a bonus everybody enjoyed. To Jennifer's deepest relief, the children granted her immense support during the separation process from their father. Eventually, after grasping the reality of their parents' marriage having been doomed to fail, they agreed in unison to be better off without a fraudster's attempt of role modelling.

I bumped into the two friends in a coffee house one day, some months after the first turbulences have settled. Emily had changed her employer by then; she found the air without Nathan around more enjoyable to breathe. Jennifer had settled into her new life as single mother with Nathan as a part-time father making appearances from time to time. When I asked if she ever had a moment of regret about her marriage having found such a stereotype end or whether she ever mourned about its fate, Jennifer just smiled. 'In hindsight, it's the best thing that ever happened to me', she replied, 'and I'm grateful for him having shown his true colours. I loved him once', Jennifer added, 'but that love was gone the moment I knew the truth. No man or relationship or even marriage is worth jeopardizing your own integrity for. Not one single man.'

What a story, and told by life. Although this might seem an extreme example of an unusual friendship forming, the number of women engaged in both sides of affairs and even ganging up against men causing their heartaches is surprisingly vast. The pain experienced by Emily and Jennifer is felt by literally hundreds of thousands of women, and the dozens of women I have worked with share the same desire for truth, independence, courage and self-confidence, plus the spirit to eliminate the male irritation for once and for all. All of them, without exception, wanted to break away from the tremendous commotion such constant pressures cause.

If you are one of these unlucky women finding yourself emotionally wedged in and blocked by an affair with a married or otherwise committed man, wrapped up in seemingly endless hours of hope, despair and never ending dreams, then think about Emily and Jennifer. Perhaps it's time to accept the likelihood to ever be anything more than just an affair in his book is slim.

Liberty anyone?
The message is short and simple – *get out.* No matter how long you have been in this make-believe relationship, it's time to finish it. To stop suffocating and manipulating your own independent future being tied up in unrealistic visions and childlike

optimism is also a good idea. You'll find your heart
and soul would truly appreciate a break from torture,
and admitting an affair is the biggest and most
damaging compromise a woman with aspirations
for a better life can make is a crucial first step.

The reason why so many women end up in this
unruly situation cannot be ignored. The fears to halt
as a leftover in our society, to remain the odd one out,
to be seen as a loser on the man-hunt front embody
very strong motivations to hook up with a man not
worth one's love and attention. A low self-esteem, a
lack of self-confidence and the foreboding of the own
conviction too often are in the way of realising true
inner potential. Despite all understandable motivation
to follow such path of wrong decision making –
a married man will never be the right choice.

Only a fairy tale
With you as his affair he most likely enjoys moments
long vanished from his matrimonial relationship –
the excitement of fresh sex, the romancing when first
intrigued with a new person, the exploring of awoken
teenage feelings together, lots of candle light dinners
with wonderful food and drink, tears of laughter when
seeing each other naked for the first time, and of course
the notorious hunter/gatherer is breaking out of him as
well. If you flatter him regularly and let him think he's
a god-like creature, he will begin to behave like one
and is smitten by his own feelings of self-importance.

In return he makes you feel special. To flesh it out
flowers, cards, more romantic dinners, long weekends

in Paris, the Cornish seaside or the Highlands of Scotland support his advances – if it looks too good to be true bear in mind it probably is, as countless women can strengthen. As long as you show signs believing his make-believe love and attention and as long as he feels safe from being caught in the act, he'll continue providing his part of the tempting fairy tale. On condition that boredom won't hit him and he replaces you with another woman – or you finish this mayhem as soon as you can – your part in this will continue until something huge, usually destroying and unconstructive, happens.

If you look at his situation from a realistic point of view you'll realise he gets the best of both worlds. The wife-world might in his eyes not further represent a fit to be seen and pure sexiness, and while introducing you to fellow humans from his social circle would equal suicide, the affair-world even now commonly functions as a trophy, smoothing his ego. This part of the affair-world signifies one of the affair's main duties. In the wife-world, he has a home where he can change his shirts and underwear, where he gets fed and has familiarity. He might have children, sharing even some sort of paternal togetherness with them. His wife, despite eventual troubles in their relationship, remains his safety net; he will invest a lot of energy into assuring this convenience won't be jeopardised.

To be the affair of a married man certainly incorporates moments of confusion; every woman who's been through this emotional dilemma will confirm this. To assist your thinking process and to support finding some answers, the following 'Question Time' will help; this exercise will aid you in finding out more about the usually evil nature of your affair. Whether the answers will be 'yes' or 'no' is not the main issue; the idea is to feed your brain some honest food for thought. With any luck, you'll find it's time to become independent and to free yourself from the overwhelming trap you're sitting in. Even more crucial, the time to realise the sincere 'you' deserves not turning wrinkly over aggravation has come.

Question Time

Have you ever caught him lying to you, whatever it might have been about and you played dull, pretending it never happened?

Have you ever caught yourself saying 'yes' to something he suggests although you felt like saying 'no'?

Have you ever felt suffocated thinking about what he's up to in his matrimonial home?

Has he ever stood you up or cancelled a dinner/trip/coffee break/theatre visit at short notice?

Does he keep mentioning he *might* leave his wife, but that he has to pick his moment wisely?

Do you find yourself staring at your mobile phone like an obsessed idiot for most of the time, especially at weekends?

Do you see any *clear* signs of him making plans to leave his wife?

Does he ever talk to you about a future together, a real future, one house, one life?

Has he ever suggested you meet his children or a member of his family?

Has he ever asked you to support him changing his life?

There could straightforwardly dozens of additional questions be listed, but these are the top ten; they are the most useful ones to assess your affair with, as they concentrate on the immediate field around your situation. It might feel daunting at first to discover certain details about suspected croakiness, but don't give in to any frustration. Many women shared similar moments, and once confronted, all women understand the sensation – illumination to the mind is best enjoyed a bit at a time. This confrontation with naked realities, even if they are unpleasant, carries some informative light only women in the discouraging position of accommodating a cheating male's overpowering testosterone level can value.

A truthful future?

When appraising your affair further, remember the most obvious – he's married, even if unhappily married; all his usual life is happening outside your bed, yet he's sleeping with you as often as he can. To keep this up, he has to practise the art of lying, regularly. In fact, it's quite shocking just how good men become at lying through their teeth without making as much as a faint whistling noise. *Can you be sure it could never happen to you?* The moment he buys himself a highly sophisticated electronic personal planner I suggest investigating further into his motives for doing so; he might be experimenting with seeing another woman in addition to you and his wife. Such busy intercourse schedule requires electronic aid. Find this is an outraging assumption? Not in my job; I have witnessed it all.

Face it – your affair is not likely to lead to anywhere permanent, other than to permanent frustration, saddened hopes, humiliating despair and countless disappointments, and you need to get out before your situation drives you mental. *How?* Just walk away; you can do that anytime you choose to do so. Once you realise you're doomed to remain in a dead-end, walking off won't be difficult.

What if he leaves his wife...?

In the unlikely event of him leaving his wife for you, justified celebrations are only in place once he proves to be faithful. I have met too many women who have raised their champagne glasses too early, having found themselves one day in the very same position the ex-wife was forced into – being betrayed. If his testosterone level keeps up, beware. Plenty of clients of mine, once having been the victims of deception themselves, confirmed to me that 'once a cheater – always a cheater' is indeed an accurate description of many inapt men.

Vital independence

Getting out is the only sensible and sovereign thing to do, and to demonstrate this independence is strongly recommended. Eventually you'll find you owe it to yourself. The importance of self-respect might have been forgotten for a while, yet it's not too late to regain it. So much more joy is linked to investing your energy finding the right man, the one you can build a relationship based on trust and understanding with. *Guilt free* enjoyment of the serenity of togetherness can then be part of a possible future. In essence, many women are victimised and lose touch with reality when the subject of 'leaving the wife' arises and are easily blinded once more. As soon as men cannot escape evocative hints of the affair any further, and providing they don't react like Nathan in the diary, openly admitting that no plans for a future together have ever been made, the cheating males appallingly often introduce plans suggesting to leave the wives in stages, a bit of break-up at a time, a couple of pounds of break-up a week. That such a suggestion is amongst the most transparent nonsense there's to be heard is needless to say.

Too big an unwholesome compromise

Let go of a dream that was never more than just a castle in the air – if you *still* think your affair is a fairy tale with a happy ending to come. Allow yourself to move on and to recognise this dream *will* inevitably turn into a nightmare. All frustrations linked to affairs are nightmares, and countless women have raised this issue during their journey towards a healthy untouchability. To be immune to men's advances

abusing women's weaknesses is a tremendous
achievement all 'former' affairs in due course
greatly care for.

Still not convinced?
If you're still driven by hope and the image of the two
of you having a fantastic life with a long term future,
there's one more question you can ask; this time not
yourself – but him. It's a fairly delicate enquiry, even
of a ridiculous nature, but has proven to be immensely
valuable enabling the tracking down of the outlined
differences his two worlds hold. Who would he save
from a burning building? Of course such incongruous
question can't be answered without questioning the
common sense of it. And he doesn't need to response
verbally – your importance is being demonstrated
every time he's leaving your bed to return home.

When being the affair becomes a habit
It's so sad, but I have met women who don't even
realise any of the negative impacts linked to being
the second woman in a man's life anymore. After
years or perhaps even decades of being 'the other
woman' some find it hard to ever imagine not living
this lie. Waiting and hoping becomes a habit, the
familiarity of sorrow creates a comfort zone (more
about this in the chapter dedicated to 'comfort zones')
and the thought of breaking out in any shape or form is
washed away vividly. In short, living this off-the-deep-
end-life, although often close to drowning, becomes
easier than declaring independence. That this view is
of course heartbreaking testament to just how many
excuses women are capable of finding is obvious.

In the end the lack of self-esteem and therefore lack of self-confidence dictate this mayhem, and the fear of having nobody is greater than having a completely inappropriate life situation. The advice to be given to the long-term dreamers is brief, especially if they state their so-called happiness publicly – *don't be fooled*.

Sooner or later this self-made distress unfortunately will catch up with life. Even after years of regularly having been pushed aside accompanying a man's convenience it wouldn't be easy to learn the true position in this man's life – latest when it comes to funeral arrangements reality will kick in. Think this is a too far in advance planning? Not in my job. I have met women, destroyed to the ground when they realised the merciless brutality of a surreal reality, women so desperate for comfort it was hard to watch, even for a professional. Not having access to the deceased drove many women I have met to breaking point, and being 'just' the affair was never felt more real and never had revealed a more devastating truth. Losing the partner of many years or perhaps even decades, even if he was a married and inappropriate man, certainly is never easy; yet unless one has ever been in this bizarre situation, no woman can possibly grasp the cruelty of this insane mayhem. Please remember, it's never too late to start living your own life, away from lies and despair. Metaphorically packing your bags and leaving, even after years and years of being the affair is possible. No woman deserves being second best, and certainly not being just a guest from a safe distance at a funeral. Bearing that in mind might trigger a long overdue awakening.

A changed world – the wife's journey

For the betrayed wives and partners, it's needless to say there's only *one* solution – discard him. It is understood that your world with only moments apart faces tremendous changes. Looking at it in a bare light, however, these changes have already taken place – just without your knowledge. The instance your husband is adulterous is the jiffy your life changes, and the very second illumination transpires is the time to turn him into fish food. *Not* to fall for any of his attempts begging for your forgiveness is non-negotiable. A man of this most foul nature does not merit tolerance. It might be tough for a while, but living without him will be the ultimate experience for you to explore. Hitting rock bottom grants a massive benefit – you can't fall any deeper; the only way being up is the logical and very liberating consequence.

Closing thoughts

Affair or wife – any second best arrangement will never be worth one's while. As the potential affair, don't fall prey, be immune to advances and flattering compliments by married or otherwise spoken for men and keep in mind the true motivation and reasons behind their behaviour. Be sharp, assess their approaches, position yourself two steps ahead – and enjoy rejecting them. To be single until the right man comes along is no crime and positively no testament to your ability to attract a male partner. To acknowledge not having found the right one just yet is part of celebrating self-acceptance and is not a quality stamp dividing women into wanted or unwanted subjects.

As the betrayed wife, notwithstanding the sorrows and pain of having lost the man you once planned your life with, accept that life holds the most bizarre revelations in stock for us. Many of them hurt, but although not always immediately noticeable, many of them also introduce untamed opportunities. Remember – too many tears age the sensitive skin around your beautiful eyes, and ulcers aren't fun to deal with, either, and certainly *no* man is ever worth such sacrifices.

Emily and Jennifer have woken up – when will you?

'Sex is as much a necessity for men as eating
chocolate is for women.
Also, both can make your hands sticky.
Unfortunately, that's where the similarities end.'

Dawn

Sex – the sticky subject

If you're lucky enough to have found the dedicated
and considering lover of your dreams and you
sincerely and genuinely have fun in the bedroom,
enjoy it as much and as often as you want and can.
You are most likely already rather experienced
in identifying your emotions, are liberated and
independent, and confident about how men tick,
so of course sex is something you therefore handle
very differently than the not so fortunate or less
experienced woman. Many women feel ok in the
bedroom and with everything is comprises, however,
some others simply don't. This chapter is devoted
to them.

For all those who feel the need for a little comfort and
support in this area, for all those who occasionally or
regularly want to run a mile, whether they are 'fakers'
or 'avoiders', let me first say that this chapter is not
intended to help women to free themselves from
sex as such. It would rather like to ease the overall
approach, the blurred or misguided vision and the
handling and experiencing of sex. It also wants to

provide food for thought about men's 'mind-world' of the subject at hand and encourage acquiring confidence as well as a true independence relating to love making. The associated dilemmas and the desire to migrate to a men-free planet, usually stemming from misunderstandings and insecurities, can be eliminated. To persuade women to stay on Planet Earth and grant a different insight to the whole matter is the idea. However, if you have, for whatever reason, decided to give up this rat race, please go directly to the very last paragraph of this chapter. Hope floats though you'll give deliverance a chance.

An important note upfront

To make one point very clear, if the man in your life happens to think you're just a handy sex appliance and he's something along the lines of hopelessly arrogant, unnervingly rude, obnoxious and ridiculous, obsessed with the constant desire to dominate, perhaps even with violent tendencies, full of even more condescension, overly self-important and suppressing others on a regular basis, full of duplicity, enjoying or toying with the idea of having affairs, either with you or others, without any consideration or respect for women or even men, possibly with an organ as small as a snapped into half French green bean, a jumbo hot dog or anything in between, to 'meet him' and 'give him' what we are about to address in this chapter is *not* the idea. As soon as you discover any of your man's attributes to include any of these bad natures, natures that do *not* deserve any understanding, let alone any support, not to mention any special sexy moments, there's only one advice to be given – never yield, and of course get out. To expose yourself to any types of male insecurities will only ever put you in a position of a guinea pig, a doormat or a sad status symbol and will cause you to lose self-respect, eventually. Unfortunately, many women find themselves in situations like these. To establish self-confidence and immunity will help to get out of any second best relationship. Men as just described are not likely to change, even if they were sent to 'male brain re-arranging boot camps', and the likelihood of him changing, even after the attempt to straighten him out, is very slim.

The overall nature of men in relationships is further discussed in 'Relationships and Men – necessity or just 'funny things'?' later in the book. For now, the men 'featured' in this chapter are nice and normal, typical and harmless, pretty innocent and also accidentally entertaining, certainly many times over misunderstood and at other times rather surprisingly lonely. In this chapter, we do not want to tackle the 'bad guys' but 'good men'. Luckily, the average man next door still represents this. This had to be clarified upfront. So let's get to work.

Divided nerves
When it comes to sex and actually mentioning the word as such, I find that people of both sexes and of all possible backgrounds, absolutely everybody pulls a face. A face with mostly at least one expression portrayed. In the case of men, we all have seen their faces when the word 'sex' is referred to, one way or another. They typically show a smiley face, paired

with some lopsidedness in the lip area, at times co-inherent with a few dribbles coming out of one corner of their mouths, and their eyes seem to become rather slitty, as if all of a sudden some ancient far eastern ancestry transpires. Once the first excitement of hearing the mention of sex has settled, male faces usually mature into an odd grin, yet still lopsided. Of course it's up to the individual's interpretation of these faces, but as far as I'm concerned they very much remind me of the rather funny Spitting Image puppets from the 1980s. These also had this interesting, slightly bare and tedious yet occupied charisma, which is hard to resist making fun of.

On the other hand, most women when mentioning sex pull faces reminding me to some extent of a solo saxophone player running out of steam but still having to play a few more notes before the next breath. The mouth seems to be forming a significantly tight and creased ring, and the eyes are wide open, representing the direct opposite to men's.

The difference in facial expression reflects the difference of the perception of sex in the two most opposites of all beings – human women and men. Legend has it that most men want it all the time and get it often enough to have turned our planet into a crowded place; another legend has it most women want to ban it, but not necessarily for environmental incentives.

When looking at its poise from a statistical point of view, almost 6.7 billion people on this planet represent, strictly speaking, at least almost 6.7 billion male ejaculations, if we ignore the few millions of twins, triplets or other multiple births for a moment. That's a huge population and a titanic number of intercourses. The invention of condoms and other pregnancy controlling devices, however, means such statistics for assessing sexual activity are no longer reliable tools. In short, heaps more is going on.

When humans are not doing it, it's on their mind. Reports suggest the male version of our species thinks about it all the time, whether the moment is appropriate or not. The same reports also imply that men automatically are assumed to have good feelings, can't wait for their next sex to take place and fantasise about it with the usual grin. When interviewed for statistical purposes, some males cared to admit of thinking of life as one long climax, unfortunately rudely interrupted by various interferences like work, the requirement to eat, the need to use the toilet or the necessity to cut the grass.

Most women don't care to share this view.

A recipe for hope
Many women I worked with who find sex to be taxing think about sex all the time, too, just from a different perspective. Various possible scenarios of how to avoid the demand for next weekend's obligatory early morning intercourse occupy their brains at the latest from Wednesday on, and the longing for a permanent solution to fix the problem dictates many moments of their active thinking time. Unfortunately, even to grasp just some brief relief from the dominating influence

of sex proves to be a degree of impossibility in our today's world.

With plentiful references of sex frequently all around us – above all noticeably exposed breasts; nicely shaped female lips and tightly dressed bottoms on TV, in newspapers or magazines; advertisements for motorbike or lorry insurances and pop videos with girls moving like starlets in a porn movie to name but a few – it's no surprise to find men being absorbed in a constant state of turn-on while women with less surgery-shaped attributes or wonky confidences on the other hand feel largely threatened by it altogether.

Over the years, the work with women who'd rather write off sex from their agendas has shown that the topic of female pleasure involved is fundamentally different to men's fascination of the matter, and of course that's no news. Finding an answer to the question 'why' became the key. Delivering a tool in disguise called 'knowledge' became that answer.

A profound insight to the world of men and their physical and mental requirements enables every woman tired of 'faking' or 'avoiding' to re-establish a healthy affiliation with sex. Despite appearances and although the appreciation of sex varies greatly, a common ground for women and men finding a path towards each other can become reality. To understand how your man ticks will provide vital knowledge, and you'll find this knowledge means power and puts you in the command seat. Being able to feel more in control when sex (and a man) is involved no longer needs to remain on your wish list, it can become a delightful reality.

Sex as subject of confusion and frustration and the reason why so many relationships fall apart or at least suffer fading harmony with the years no longer has to be an enemy. In a way you never thought sex can become your ally.

Example: one show – two views
Contrary to many women's liking, men paying attention towards sex and sexy details are fed throughout our daily life. Sex sells, it ensures awareness and keeps male brains busy, even if only on a one-dimensional level. To draw in male audiences, even cookery programmes on TV, the least of all places one should suspect, show female presenters with see-through blouses or too tight t-shirts. With an attention span limited to displayed female attributes, no further consideration for the tips and tricks on how to create the perfect Pavlova or the easiest chicken stock is granted.

The offended and aggravated woman sitting next to the man with the miraculously found interest in cooking, when duly lacking self-confidence or awareness, only wants to do one thing – to switch of the black box and read a book, preferably without being exposed to any mention of sex.

Her own drawbacks and issues circle her mind, her aversion to sex reminds her of the morning's encounter, the sense of disappointment is fuelling to dread the next time. Her concerns don't receive any support from a world full of hints of a subject which made her man concentrate on a cookery programme.

One a plus side, some fifteen years ago consumer psychologists have communicated to the profit driven industry of the western shopping world the potential of men's constant desire for signs of arousal, initiating big corporations' implementation of window display mannequins to have hints of erected nipples, the 'dolls' usually 'wearing' tight pieces of clothing. Studies have proven men's willingness to part with money lots more easily and lots more happily when surrounded by persistent nipple action, even if only experienced on a piece of plastic.

The rift

Discontented women's ideas of how to handle men with healthy testosterone levels range from castrating all males and to only keep a few for insemination, via mincing them and selling the meat to local fisheries to shooting them off into space with an exceptionally powerful rocket. In a nutshell, nine out of ten women I have met were unhappy with their sex life, especially once the children were born. This number is shockingly high.

Almost half of those who'd like to escape sex would jump up in joy, cheering aloud even, if sex was out of their lives. Men, of course, would commit mass suicide if that was ever to happen.

The other half of restless women would rather run a Marathon, totally unfit and without trainers if need be, and would find themselves more alive running with bleeding feet rather than contributing any enjoyable activities in the bedroom. I believe it's a relief to communicate that the desire for offspring at least opens the mind to the necessity to team up in this matter; both sexes agree on this, and we should celebrate this rare unison.

Depressing fact is that sex causes more friction between two people than any other subject, closely followed by financial struggle. One might be the richest person in the world, if one's sex life is out of balance unhappiness sooner or later strikes, even if one could buy sexual attention. If one has no financial means to live a jet setter lifestyle but has established a beautiful bedroom bond with a partner of their choice, the lack of money often seems to diminish to nothing more than a slightly bothersome issue. To have both would of course be some sort of height of fortune for many.

The catalogue of grounds why women would rather avoid the topic and activity is cosmic. It ranges from suffering the feeling of being used like a public convenience, to feeling emotionally misunderstood, to experiencing a lack of male communication, to facing an overall lack of compatibility with the counterpart and last but not least to accommodate the never fading pressure of having to like the male's attempt of bliss delivery. These are indeed the top five reasons women feel gloomy in the bedroom. If one asks 1,214 women about their sexual challenges one gets 1,214 different explanations, but in quintessence these top five get a mention. You'd also find 1,214 different ways of coping, with faking 'things' to be the most common way of dealing with the inflicted stress of sex. One could say women the world over turned into promising thespians all around.

Many women also confirm that if there wasn't 'that thing' to be dealt with on Sunday mornings or Bank Holiday afternoons, after the football, the relationship with the man of their choice would be quite pleasant. True love felt for a man does in a woman's book not necessarily equal getting sweaty – togetherness embodies the significance.

The major woman-man difference is to be discovered in the perception of sex. Most women on the quest for a better awareness of the matter describe their desire for bedroom noise only as an extra in their life, as some sort of bonus if it happens but not as a necessity, like men typically illustrate their needs. The gap between women's reality and men's inevitability causes added friction when the two parties involved feel under any type of pressure – and both parties do.

Nature's purpose, some necessity and today's reality
Although always suspected, it usually comes as a surprise to many women that sex is indeed a necessity for men as any other human activity like eating, sleeping, drinking and breathing signifies – with one exception: despite men's commonly known analysis of this, it is not mandatory to physically survive. We all need to eat, sleep, drink and breathe or sooner rather than later we would die. Without climaxes, the

male body is totally capable of survival; it might drive men's mind up the wall or make them eat weird food combinations like cucumbers with strawberry ice cream, but apart from indigestion no lethal danger to men's life would arise.

The word 'necessity' has to be understood as the degree of men's preferences when given a choice between eating and experiencing ecstatic physical fulfilment. It is the one activity men would chose over eating or perhaps even breathing at any time, if only they could. This powerful drag, imposed by nature, men quite simply cannot resist. Mature versions of the male species subject this pull to the influence of willpower, an art younger men still have to acquire. The implication of 'necessity', however, applies to all ages. To reach the climax is the overall purpose, for baby making as well as for pleasure, and without it the bustle loses its principle. *This perception is not even men's fault.*

Nature was very clear, enormously practical and incredibly clever with this design. It assures the continuous existence of our species. The necessity of climaxes for men, programmed by Mother Nature, meets the necessity of many women to have children. If we forget about the modern woman for a moment and go far back to prior our so-called civilised society, women had not much at all to have and to-hold – other than babies, children, off-spring. They were their capital, they were what only they could produce and deliver, and it simply reinforced an easier survival.

For many thousands of years females have continuously exchanged sex and children for food and shelter, and at times of hardship for other supplies. Sex is the one meaning women could rely on; its use became intuitive instinct. The desire to have children was conveniently met by the desire of men to enjoy best moments; the number of children in older times also bearing testament to any one man's wealth. Some rural tribes still follow this model in their society today. The very simple design of men's desire of one sort meeting women's desires of another sort guaranteed that even not so sanctified females were blessed with children. Everybody was taken care of.

With Nature's blueprint as the base, both sides always get what they are programmed to desire. Nowadays, however, most of us don't live in caves but in the modern world, and after centuries of struggle women these days can enjoy their views to be considered of relevance, and the need for a woman to have children in order to make herself interesting is no longer given, is no longer her only way to obtain food or shelter, in short is no longer crucial as means for survival.

Today, women are somewhat expected to view sex exclusively as pleasure of higher grounds, especially after the children are born. Men won't stop wanting what nature has blessed them with, just because the name-carrying offspring are out of nappies. Back in the old days, a woman hardly ever had to worry about sex being a source of joy; the intercourse activity was a mere method to deliver babies; no further attention or significance was granted. Men certainly never wasted any thought on whether or not any female pleasure was part of this amusement, but neither did the women. They were usually worried about pregnancies and worked very hard to make sure their fragile young stayed alive. Very much a fact in our today though is the verity that many women, now the necessity to trade in babies for food and shelter has vanished almost completely from our lives, do not have fun doing 'it'. The face and purpose of sex has changed.

Today's women *want* to enjoy sex as much as men do, and more so than they ever did in the history of womankind – the fact that this desire hasn't yet widely found fulfilment is attestation for the fundamental disparity between women and men. One aim – but a thousand misunderstandings.

Too many great expectations or down-to-earth realism?
What modern women crave according to Hollywood's and innumerable singer-songwriter's understandings can be found impicted in countless romantic movies and thousands of lyrics. Every generation had their sex bombs and studs and a capturing story to go with them; they all carry dreams and accounts of women's desires.

When analysing films and music referring to women's needs, apparently all ladies seek slow hands, an easy touch, someone with time, with the sexual wisdom of Greek gods, and the willingness to listen to the female body, totally forgetting or rather controlling their own aspirations and perhaps even their needs.

When analysing women's comprehension of this theme, one finds women realised ages ago that the skilful, understanding, mature, slow handed and soft lipped lover is as rare a find as a flawless diamond. They exist, sure, but they are a rarity, and today's women's expectations slowed accordingly. Taking this as base, Hollywood clearly will continue to see the profitable potential of fairytale movies and will simply continue to produce these. In moments of enjoying some relieving escapism we all hunt for some love and affection, protection and limitless lovers, even if it was just on the big screen.

Away from cinema shows, the accurate outlook of the modern average woman on bedroom activities is relatively down-to-earth and blessed with reserve. A lover willing to take a little overall interest in the female psyche when it comes to sex, even if it was only a diminutive curiosity, is already considered a great find.

As Hollywood suggests quite rightly, in our dreams and in an ideal world we all want the loving, caring, knowing, willing, slow enough, kissing, massaging, caressing, funny, devoted, determined, committed and understanding lover, but in reality not all of these characteristics are incorporated in any one man. Many of women's devotees are far from it, and they watch Hollywood's interpretations of their ladies preferences in agony, very aware of their own limits. The likelihood that a man shows up in one's life with *all* tempting qualities is as rare as the flawless diamond is itself. Luckily, and despite their own discontentment most modern women have come to terms with this.

Pressure kills pleasure

Men want to make love. In essence, even those women who'd love to leave the planet want to make love, too. The difference at the bottom line is that men, however, can't quite see the relevance of sex unless they in due course reach the highest ground of physical satisfaction, as it otherwise seems pointless to physically exhaust oneself and not redeem some sort of reward for it at the end.

Many women, on the other hand, classify reaching a climax as a bonus, merely as an extra not occupying the rank of inevitability. Very much the contrary is the case. Most women I have worked with experienced nothing but pressure deriving from the whole business of ecstatic climax reaching. What might bear a quality of joy perception, the pleasure of togetherness, of sharing special moments is eclipsed by the burden to show predictable signs of seventh heaven. Unless women begin to communicate this aspect, misunderstandings, the urge to migrate, the wish to vanish and mastering the exhausting art of faking pleasure, joy and entertainment is cruelly awaiting. Unhappiness for women is eminent, and men's opinion about women's killjoys is illustrious. Before the parties become aware, the rift between the two sexes widens. While accusing each other, some suffer silently, some shout their distresses aloud in a battle of swear words, in addition women accuse men of selfishness and men accuse women of emotional recklessness. *But there's hope.*

The enlarged pressure on women forms a sensitive barrier of underestimated proportions. The more women find themselves exposed to sexual stress, the more they will recoil. Men are left with the misery of feeling misunderstood or worse, fearing the woman in their life might be sexually unfulfilled. The one or the other Hollywood hero springs to mind and both sides experience demonstrative havoc.

When sex works it represents one of the most critical bonds between two people; in fact it's a bond so influential that it requires constant stimulation. When experienced with joy and mutual agreement and understanding, it pads the path of any relationship with flowers; not necessarily virtually, but certainly spiritually.

To achieve this is every persons wish – but the accomplishment rests pretty much on strong female shoulders. My work has revealed that women respond to fixing these kinds of challenges more efficiently than men, that factual statements and information are intuitively processed on a level of diverse maturity. However, the key to attain this is knowledge - the female wisdom and expertise of men's nature. Once women understand their budding influence on any bedroom pleasures, taxing misunderstandings and unnecessary frictions fade away.

Not just men's responsibilities
Since it being quintessentially in their DNA, men love to have lots of the pleasure nature programmed them to want. The female partner in crime is left with the challenge of having to choose between surrender to male advances while feeling dreadful or to oppose

certain desires and face the destruction of any already fragile harmony.

To automatically assume the female frame of mind is positively associated with masculine sexual talents or, in fact, the lack of it, sees males' supposed skills suffer unfair prejudice which even men don't deserve.

Despite the general acceptance to *not* have a Hollywood hero in the domestic bedroom, many pressured women still at times are quick to blame their men for the misery. Too often this deepens the discrepancies in perceiving sexual bliss; to think 'things' are entirely men's fault is as unreasonable as men's criticism of women only ever being interested in soap operas, shoes, handbags, lipsticks or chocolate cup cakes.

Aiming to be modern and independent women, we also have to take responsibility in this department and have to admit it takes two to input the best possible for a good and harmonic outcome. Often blame and the fear to address a problem mix unhealthily, leaving women in a lone mood and men misunderstood once more. Fact is men can only be as good in bed as the training they received for it. A few courageous men have, quite rightfully, used this wisdom to describe their very own grief in the bedroom. Not many want to admit it, but a few brave warriors hold the male flag up high, praying for deliverance.

All of a sudden, pressure is not limited to female awareness. While women feel under pressure to enjoy themselves, men feel under pressure to deliver joy. It's a very strange vicious circle, constantly fuelled by confusion and quarrels. Basically, both women and men want the same, however, until the obstructed views of both parties involved are cleared, the circle will keep on spinning.

Since placing blame is usually easier than accepting some responsibilities, many women I have worked with accidentally fell into a bad habit of doing so, resulting in men becoming immune to blame and women blocking fulfilling sex out of their lives. Whether you become a 'faker' or an 'avoider' is somewhat determined by your degree of annoyance to address the subject. 'Fakers' usually consider themselves still part of the game, while 'avoiders' have mastered the art of finding excuses and have given up playing altogether.

Fact is men are not automatically heroes in bed just because nature releases a never drying up flow of testosterone into their bloodstream. Overall, it takes two to make the difference between good and bad bedroom noise. Misunderstandings, embarrassments and prejudice happen too often, which puts everybody under unnecessary pressure. It can't be and isn't just a one-way street. Also, nothing is ever edged in stone when it comes to sex. Bear in mind that your man isn't born with any insider information or a manual explaining your sexual preferences attached to his chest. How you tick, what you fancy and what you resent in bed is for you to communicate. To blame him for not being able to read your mind won't contribute towards any positive development.

The often absent communication about 'the' subject
also never helps. Nine out of ten couples simply
never, or in insufficient detail, discuss their worries.
Too many views and ideas, talents and curiosities
are left in the dark; guesswork and presumption
take place where honest discovery paired with a
few good laughs about how the two of you look in
a doctor's and a nurse's outfit should be happening
instead.

Being good in bed is *not* a gift received upon birth.
I have heard countless women saying because their
male partner wasn't experienced in bed they wouldn't
enjoy sex. Think again. Sex needs to be taught – and
learnt – like walking and talking needs attention in
order to be mastered.

This goes for women, too.

A good old, not too demanding chat
To 'teach' your man some tips and tricks will most
likely open a whole new horizon for you, too.
What is going on in your head and in your body
will introduce him to your side of the story as well
as give you an opportunity to learn about yourself.
Expressing that you understand *his* version of nature's
intent is your ally to establish a new level
of compatibility between the two of you. Good things
evolve from verbal communication, so make a start,
open your mouth and talk. Pick your moment wisely;
avoid 'lager space' or 'quality bloke time' or 'the
footie', which are all times when he's not paying a
great deal of attention to anything else. When the

time is right, teach him about sex the way women think – women in general and you in particular. Gather the courage to express what you dislike; wrapping it up in a factual manner won't leave your man feeling criticised, which is crucial. You need not be embarrassed; take into account him possibly being even more uncomfortable than you are.

Over the years the best tactic to introduce one's man to the topic of sex from a female point of view, is essence outlining the foremost differences between the two sexes, proved to be the relief of pressure having to give a superstud performance. To explain that women don't appreciate having to fake enjoyment is the next important step. To further explain that you indeed understand Mother Nature's design of compulsory pleasure-seeking in men delivers another central basis.

Since verbal communication is unfortunately *not* part of the DNA of the average male, the step by step approach to introducing your man to pressure-free love making is strongly suggested. This move towards better understanding proves to hold awakening benefits to men's curiosities. A fact often underestimated when judging men's attention spans. Even the most hopeless cases will eventually enter a conversation on an adult level, if you're lucky. To introduce the following simplest of all routines to your life will relieve any pressures of both of you. To remind you, the whole idea behind this chapter is to improve your sex life, providing this is what you would like to at least consider.

Long term solution – <u>no</u> agenda

Our lives are full of timetables, deadlines, journals, records, logs, diaries, appointments, chronicles, calendars, intervals, schedules – the very last factor women, or men, wish for their sexual manners and moods, desires and dreams is to be driven by any sort of agenda.

Agendas linked to romantic activities will limit your mood, ambush your objective perception and merely sabotage your fun in the bedroom. To *not* have an agenda is strictly speaking the only rule one ever needs to obey. 'No agenda' means no pressure. 'No agenda' means taking matters easy. 'No agenda' means relaxing without any expectations from either side. 'No agenda' means relief and honesty. 'No agenda' is a heart-to-heart of two people feeling openness between them. 'No agenda' means if higher grounds can be reached, that's great, if not, that's fine, too. 'No agenda' means trust and understanding. As soon as women empathise this, this revelation can be delivered to the lucky lover. It's time men appreciate that pillow talk is no Olympic discipline.

So, in plain words – explain to the man of your desire 'being together' bears more importance to you than 'coming together'; communicate that not feeling the need to 'go all the way' does not automatically equal him being a romantic failure, but simply reflects your physical mood. It's identical to the offer of ice-cream, but not being tickled by it in that very instance. Re-assurance is a vital ally at this point to avoid emotional frustration on his side.

'Faker' or 'avoider' in women's cases as well as men fearing to oppose to Hollywood's visions, once women deliver the eye-opener to their men and both sexes accept the differences, the subject of making love can be fun without having to sell a female fake or driving males into physical exodus. The sympathetic tolerance of 'him' and 'his best friend' is the next way point.

The troubled man

As many have always somewhat assumed, for the average man to reach a climax is a compulsive impulse. Sexual fulfilment is the highest priority on his wish list of expectations when in a relationship even if he politely denies it when being asked. Him wanting 'it' and convincing you to accommodate 'it' is in his genes and therefore not really his fault. Bearing that in mind makes us women hopefully understand our men a bit better and see their constant subjecting of what seems like an obsession with sex a little less selfish.

Just remember, he can't but want sex, even if he resembles a mature version of the species and celebrates his success of controlling his needs more effectively. He still would love to have 'it'. Males not quite strong enough to manipulate their urges come across as a little too strong at times. Nature does the best she can to ensure our continued existence. Once men learn not to fear a doomed deprivation of the most influential itch in their lives, they'll calm down eventually.

In their ideal dream world, men would be studs in the bedroom, would love to give us ladies a great

time and would love to be admired for it as well.
Some men put themselves under a lot of pressure,
constantly comparing themselves to clichés and
forcing themselves to differentiate between 'good' and
'bad'. Only men can come up with such evaluation.

Fearing the own limits in bed is amongst the worst
challenges the easily broken male psyche ever has to
cope with. Countless guys are haunted by images
of women in ecstasy, ridiculous pornographic
interpretations of female delight and their own male
wishful thinking. The anxiety some men stretch to as
a result of these ludicrous influences is alarming, to
say the least. Men insist reputation must be at stake.
The faint and mistaken analysis of women's actual
involvement in the matter doesn't help either.

Men love to be admired, although not always just for
their hideous cars with hideous exhaust pipes and
hideous spoilers driving along at hideous speed.
It's sad, but this collection of excessive motorsport
material and race driver behaviour is one of the biggest
indicators of a man's self-image in the bedroom. Any
lack of admiration or indeed self-confidence they feel
the desire to hide is expressed in the nature of their
unsightly vehicles.

Men also love to feel needed, wanted and desired as
the next person; the male way of communicating these
wishes is simply stranger and often reaches deranged
magnitudes. Only a few ever are man enough to admit
that being a man in today's world is not an easy task.
The introduction of pressure relief, in men's cases not

having to perform a miracle, in women's cases not having to make mewing noises, is the common ground to regroup on. It will also prove beneficial for the wallet, as less and less car parts will be necessary.

To establish communication as new collateral into the relationship is crucial, however, bringing up the subject of 'sex' without patronising male's ears and certainly without belittling the male delicate psyche indicates a true challenge. Men don't often learn as easily as dogs do, although polite blackmailing with food has done the trick once or twice.

Strategic input is to show support. Expressing your kind and tolerant understanding of the most important factor for him – him and his sex drive – is fundamental. He needs to understand that no threat is being felt, that no blame will fall on him, that no ultimatum will be set, that no selfishness is responsible. Indicate your objective support and awareness of nature's design and deliver the pressure-relief at one simple swoop. Once he gets over the initial shock and realises he's in male heaven, it's the perfect moment to relief him further of any other outstanding worries – his performance between sheets and your judgement of it. The time to introduce the female point of view on sexual fulfilment and the perplexing differences between the sexes has come. At the latest at this point men have developed a previously unknown talent for listening.

A new dimension
The next step after this revelation is to demonstrate your unique understanding in a way most women

find repelling or even offending and outraging in the early stages of this learning process. However, my years working with women in similar situations – in spite of it probably being the oddest and atypical, rather rare and surely least expected advice you could ever receive regarding the whole subject – have proven this approach to be of immense assistance in deciphering emotional hieroglyphics caused by two-way sexual pressure. The suggestion is simple – practically, literally and virtually give your man what he needs – sex.

The plan and purpose for this is to establish a new motivation to include positive sex into your relationship again. You need not be alarmed; understanding your man and showing it accordingly does *not* turn you into a sex toy, a cheap slapper or a convenience.

What often is initially seen as strange symbolises the command seat which was briefly referred to at the beginning of this chapter; it bears one simple fact – saying 'yes' is more rewarding than saying 'no' – *as long as you set the rules, at your terms and conditions.*

As long as you dictate the timing and the extent of your bedroom activities you will feel in complete control. Only you know what mood you're in and therefore only you decide how far the game of discovery goes. For him to not make the first move is essential – it would turn the tables of decision making, a fact most women resent. 'Gentle female power' is the secret. The open-minded and willing to learn man will join in your game without questioning your motives. Since you relieved him of any pressures to deliver the sometimes impossible or unnecessary and communicated your understanding of his perception as well as your view point of the matter in general, this pressure-free zone all of a sudden extends towards your own emotions and can provide a whole fresh game of joy altogether. 'No agenda' will work wonders – you might even decide to join him in pleasure-*taking*. The possibilities are endless; to use one's imagination has proven to be a supreme source. Overall, this approach combines your being in charge with him grinning uncontrollably – no pressure certainly opens pristine views and the willingness to learn.

This applies to both sexes.

Real happy endings – not just Hollywood
Your involvement on this novel level will most likely contribute indeed towards a new dimension within your man. For a start, most men appreciate and cherish the thought of not having to endure prolonged efforts of ice-cream serving, when indeed ice-cream is not desired at the moment. Not having to face the risk of a heart attack triggers feelings of great relief, too; this serves as added bonus. You, on the other hand, can relax from now on. If you feel like 'it', you'll let him know. If you don't feel like 'it', that's fine, too. As long as you demonstrate your understanding of Mother Nature's design on him, he's always going to be calm and comforted.

The most interesting side effect of two-way pressure elimination is the occurrence of sudden curiosities and novelties. This phenomenon usually materialises within the first few shy endeavours. The more relaxation is allowed to take place the more all senses heighten. You'd be amazed, as many women have been before you. The unusual and gentle line of sexy attack delivers ease for both parties to enjoy and is certainly worth a shot.

The rest is up to you.

An important footnote
If your man has any medical issues in the area of sexual health, address them together and seek medical advice from a qualified and certified professional. Many women are simply unaware of their men's problems, let alone their need for medical attention. Show your support the best you can by making his problems yours and stand by him with all the re-assurance you can give. Once he's over his shyness, he'll appreciate your concern and help.

Another important footnote
If you find yourself at a waypoint in your life where the whole lovemaking business, however explanatory and enlightening this chapter might have been, doesn't hold any attraction for you anymore, if you find yourself developing an understanding for your man but even more so an understanding for yourself –

so be it, but being honest about it is for reasons of fairness towards the male part of the union strictly speaking non-negotiable. It's strongly recommended to openly communicate your feelings as soon as appropriate. I have met a huge number of women who, after experimenting for a while and despite all willingness to grant sympathy, came to the decision to not engage in bedroom noises any further, for good.

Hormonal changes in the female body are usually responsible, and no one is to blame – they simply take place and coincide with various side effects, one of them being a total lack of sex drive. Women I have worked with in this situation have initiated their relationships with truly beloved men to exclude any physical aspects more or less from one day to the next. Courage is vital to communicate this, as could be expected. It's also strongly advised to give significant consideration to the male partner involved, as for him such state of mind is totally alien. Sex is what most men are born to want *and* get, one way or another. To combine your choice of freedom with his essential desires you'd have to make your relationship a platonic one, solely based on companionship, and follow your instincts, yet allow him to follow his. To *not* be upset, annoyed or irritated if he scans other women, either on TV or in real life, from top to toe is part of the deal once the two of you have settled for 'platonic', and the entitlement to criticise him following his impulses is invalidated in due course.

Most men are utterly shocked at first to find themselves exposed to, in their view, such an unfair circumstance; however, many eventually accept the nature of the game of female progression, mostly, of course, because they have no choice. If the relationship is doomed to crash, it might trigger a break-up; scratching sex off the list of activities will show how weak or strong a relationship outside the bedroom is. If the relationship is strong enough in its sum, mutual understanding might stand a decent chance.

If your man finds himself happily involved with your personality and the life the two of you share, the world won't necessarily end if lovemaking ends. Other ways to bond can be found; regular cuddles or always holding hands, a deep chat or simply being there for the other person can move mountains. There are ways for a male to find physical satisfaction without engaging in silly affairs or facing bankruptcy hiring sex traders. All there's to be done is to establish an open mind and a mutual understanding for each other's preferences.

As before, the rest is up to you.

'After all the trouble you go to,
you get about as much actual 'food'
out of eating an artichoke as you would from
licking 30 or 40 postage stamps.'

Miss Piggy

Diets – the shortest piece of advice ever written?

The myth of diets to be the right long-term solution to solve hefty weight issues refuses to die. Thousands and thousands of books, online advice, group meetings and various other systems on the subject fill worldwide consumer circuses, especially in the western world, and are testament of the overwhelming and overpowering importance 'diets' symbolise.

As briefly mentioned at the beginning of this little book of freedom, too many 'how to', in this case 'how to lose weight' books weigh too heavily in one's hands. Numerous women I have worked with confirm the density of various approaches on how to shift excess body mass to be wearing, tiring, confusing, too complicated, inefficient and hope-cracking. Endless cycles of information are said to cause information overflow without gaining any inside to the subject at hand, and the issue of 'diets' is the perfect example of how to make things more complicated than they have to be. With an overly saturated market, and backed by countless women, the hungry need for simple, brief, straightforward and comprehensible advice has emerged.

While thousands and thousands of pages could easily fill this chapter, it distances itself to join in the long debate about the 'rights' and 'wrongs' in the daily battle with weight and certainly refuses to repeat already established information covering obesity, New Year's resolutions, health risks, the body's survival mode when deprived of food, slow metabolism, the importance of exercise and vanity related advice. Instead, it's pleasantly and insanely short, easily accessible, and direct food for thought fills its crest – most likely possibly offering the shortest piece about 'diets' ever written.

Diets, as they are commonly known, millions of women concerned can and would happily confirm this, do *not* work long-term in the battle against the bulge. If any of them were useful the world wouldn't be swamped with diet books or diet systems. Every new book or system on the subject will only ever add to the long list of the try-fail-try-again-fail-again cycle. The emotional cage this cycle symbolises is so powerful and influential it drove many women I have met wandering towards collapse, of mentally packing in, of migrating to a different planet yet again, away from dress sizes being seen as verification to a lifestyle choice rather than factual information about a woman's DNA dictated measurements.

To make matters worse, the dire influences mass media channels abuse to get to women in the situation of being pleasantly chubby by using more than foul mind games are shocking, and if there was such a thing as 'morally illegal', this would be it. Bulimia, anorexia, yo-yo dieting – many women I have worked with have experienced these dreadful side-effects and every woman ever been exposed to these can confirm their misery.

The bottom line is simple – for far too long diets have taken over women's responsibilities to take care of any weight issues. The ability of independent decision making is impaired by one diet or another and yet another because they keep on failing us. Leaving the decision to others, i. e. diets about what and what not to eat, when to eat and what exercise regime to follow has left many blinded to the fact that the own life should be lived sheltered from such absurd influences. Diets claim to know the human body – and soul – while in fact only a handful of these facts have been clinically proven to be universal on all women alike.

Well known, involuntarily and frequently explored emotional cages called 'diets' and 'images', paired with unhealthy compromises called 'expectations' and 'stereotypes' don't send any shock waves of surprise towards those women who have at any one time been on this path of ridiculous promises made by diets, disappointed hopes caused by realism, mind-blowing frustration triggered by hunger, doomed resolutions facing the lack of willpower and an empty basket of wishful thinking. Increasingly frequent abuse of women's desire to improve their self-image in front of the mirror drives women the western world over into toying with the idea of jumping into a pool filled with gallons of acidic liquid. *More than ever, the time to receive liberation from excruciatingly absurd diet promises has come.*

The advice is, yet again, simple – ditch diets as means to control your body mass for once and for all. Stop handing over your responsibility to meet, for example, important health issues. To get back into the driver's seat and to dictate the road one's driving on is the only way out of this heavy mess.

Abused hopes, ridiculous promises and never-ending frustration about the subject of weight loss don't have to dictate one's day-to-day life. An overpowering consumer psychology will always be around us – to grow immune against it is the objective. Decades of dietary advice offered to the overweight on a huge scale have created a massive catalogue of strategies on how to play with the desperate human mind. To ignore such mind games is strongly recommended; the normal human emotion of 'hope' for a quick-fix on weight matters as well as other blindingly tainted ways to get one to part with money, purchasing yet another diet idea, is their quest. This quick-fix, as millions have independently worked out without obtaining a degree in psychology first, does not exist. *Using diets is useless.*

Instead, *use common sense.* This is the only advice you'll ever need to follow, therefore it's most likely the shortest 'diet' advice you'll ever receive. The word 'diet', by the way, in its origins in the old Latin and

Greek worlds, bears no resemblance with 'losing weight' – diet means lifestyle. If being sensible is a diet, so be it.

This easy, sensible method eliminates the need for any other line of attack. If eating pizza at eleven o'clock at night before going to bed isn't sensible, don't do it. If eating a full Sunday Roast after a brisk walk to the pub is sensible, enjoy it. If having four instead of two bars of chocolate isn't sensible, don't have four. If enjoying a couple of pieces of double-layered chocolate cake first thing in the morning after dancing all night long with the girls on an uplifting night out, tuck in. If eating a leftover butter croissant just before going out for dinner isn't sensible, don't eat it. If it's sensible to incorporate more fruit and vegetables, watch fat and water intake, follow this sensible guideline. It can't get any easier, requires no financial commitment, can be implemented into any daily routine – and being in charge feels good, too. In short, *if it's sensible, eat it – if it's not sensible, don't eat it.*

Any woman, virtually anybody, treating food with this effortless common-sense-approach introduced in this short chapter will find great relief feeling responsible about the own well-being again. No further daunting and doomed to fail diet systems are necessary to achieve a long longed for hale and hearty health – and weight. All books about diets on a shelf at home will now only be good for gathering dust. Not to give them away to charity is charitable – the myth of diets to be the tool against weight gain deserves to be bunged up. As far as exercise is concerned, it supports weight loss, of course; however, to be sensible about food intake without facing ridiculous physical training works, too. Weight loss happens without it, but simply slower.

All women I have introduced to this food for thought, all those who were seeking deliverance from the endless vicious circles of promising diets and disappointing dieting, without exception those women were initially gazing at me as if I were a mental lunatic needing some sort of straightjacket and medication assisted rescuing from myself. After years of brainwashing manipulation such simple advice, perhaps too simple to be working, was considered to be gobbledygook in many ears. Miraculously, the women trying this madcap approach suggested by their life coach have discovered it worked. A freed mind became the most important achievement, extra weight fell off and 'the spooky catch' is still being looked for. For once, 'if it looks too good to be true' is *not* applicable. However, don't take my word for it, try it for yourself.

Limiting emotional cages, for many a second skin, can finally be shed without losing faith on the way, and anybody finding this advice too short to be effective should simply read this chapter over and over again to make it appear longer.

A sneak preview – self-acceptance and <u>real female beauty</u>
Sustaining a healthy weight, for various reasons, is of course desirable; if, however, no strong medical indications are given and one is perfectly healthy

with a stone or two or more too many and in addition
upliftingly happy with life itself – enjoy life and
what it might hold in stock for you. Curvy females
like Caroline Quentin, Dawn French, Alison Moyet,
Roseanne Barr, Margaret Rutherford, Miss Piggy
and many others certainly never seemed
victimised by their cuddly and pleasantly chubby
female attributes; to the naked eye, their body
mass never stood in the way of their impressive
achievements.

Anybody ever having witnessed the mesmerising
aura of a curvy woman walking into a festive room,
carrying her body filled with a relaxed and healthy
attitude, with a winning and capturing smile, simply
knowing she looks gorgeous, will agree that the dress
size is the least bit affecting any charisma; true
feminine beauty shines through the self-acceptance
being of weight some health or other organisations
care to brand doomed.

Many studies have proven women as described
here are considered many times over more attractive
than women half the size festering in the corner of a
cheerful venue as far away as possible from any food
on offer. The thought of not being able to enjoy what
is strictly speaking a healthy crave drives Miss Skinny
into grumpiness easily detectable by all others sharing
the same space, by women and men alike. The curvy,
self-confident woman might be twice the size in
weight, yet all eyes are on the *true* beauty only truly
self-confident women can communicate to the outer
world by shimmering and bursting with two

invincible virtues – amazing inner independence and untouchable self-acceptance. Men especially, of all ages, sizes and backgrounds, would willingly and in a much earnest state of mind confirm this sexy fact, and the dictation to be skinny or even 'only' slim for others to sense sensuality is yet another myth. Discovering this tiny fact forces happiness to follow in due course on the journey to self-acceptance.

Curvy Miss Piggy always knew it; food is a too good a fun factor to miss out on; who's sensible with food will never need a diet system of any nature, and no sacrifice will ever have to be faced again. Depriving oneself is a nuisance of the past and practising the art of self-acceptance lifts any woman in eager demand for a happier life to previously unknown higher grounds.

Bon appétit.

'I've always thought my philosophy
should be never to start
and always to finish a fight with my husband's ex;
that was until I realised there's actually neither a
reason nor a need to fight.
It's odd in which mysterious corners of life friends
can be found.'

Donna

The ex – factor

Considering the amount of hatred and disgust linked
to the 'ex' all around, one can't but express surprise
about the limited number of homicides taking place
based on this fact. Hardly any emotion seems more
powerful than the detestation of the former woman,
friend, lover and partner in the own man's life. When
children are involved, especially when new, now
united children arrive, the real fun and battle for love,
attention and money seems to start.

I lost count about how many women I have met over
the years expressing the mad desire to slice through
the throat of the own man's 'ex'. Apart from the newly
adopted hobby of sharpening knives, the lengthy
plans, timetables and agendas planning some stalking
or other observation activities to gain a better insight
to the life and daily routines of the 'ex' by many of
the 'new' women have never seized to amaze me.
Great efforts are being invested into inspecting the

alleged enemy, at times with precisions worthy
a strategic planner's position in the British Army.

When asked 'why do you do any of this?' most women
would look at me rather surprised, to say the least,
clearly asking themselves why I would come up with
such a silly question. 'I have to be two steps ahead of
her, don't I?' is what I usually received for an answer.
In fact, many of my clients in the position of being
the 'new' woman indeed visualised the 'ex' to be
an enemy of most foul proportions. Worries and
suspicions of various bizarre natures were assumed
around anything that ever had to do with the infamous
'ex'. To ever think of the 'ex' as perhaps a friend
instead of just a foe was utterly unthinkable for most
and any unexpected suggestions I have made in this
direction were at first of course, and not surprisingly,
discarded with blooming disgust. The naked fact that
the 'ex' might just be a harmless fellow woman not
sharing the urge to use sharp knives initially seems
alien to many 'new' women.

Surveys have shown the 'ex', ex as in ex-wife, ex-
partner or ex-girlfriend, is considered by countless
women to be one of the biggest threats to an
otherwise pleasant and intact relationship. Many of
my female clients have looked for liberating and
assisting advice for years; countless books, lots of
DVD's and even self-help groups available to ease
the pain caused by the 'ex' most women have found
to have one thing in common – they deliver the
same *questionable* advice; an advice not suitable for
providing any long-term and smooth deliverance.

To 'grow a thick skin' or 'to re-group the inner strength and fight to the mattresses' are the most often given counsels; even some of my peers recommend the slicing option – metaphorically speaking. Frankly, this fancy but empty advice, in my book, however, does nothing but add to the confusion many women struggle with when the subject of the 'ex' raises either reasonable or unreasonable concerns and worries.

This overall approach to fight and to struggle, to grow thick skin and to re-group, to quarrel and to disagree with anything concerning the 'ex' seems to have mutated into a very bad habit. Without giving it any great deal of thought women automatically assume the 'ex' can't but be horrible, annoying, destructive and vicious. Many women don't even know the 'ex' in person, know nothing whatsoever about their qualities or challenges. Most 'new' women only ever catch a brief glance of the 'ex' from a distance, yet too many feel very free to brand the 'ex' as bitch or witch or worse, both. The true nature of the 'ex' remains as hidden as some men's willingness to fill the 'new' woman in on the past.

The own man's account therefore and usually exclusively lays the foundations of the 'new' woman's view on how to perceive the 'former' woman. The 'ex' being the 'ex' naturally won't receive too much praise from the man, even if she were the most beloved woman on the planet or the only true love in their lives – men are not that stupid. Knowing instinctively it could cause them trouble, men usually aim high but fly low when the subject of the 'ex' comes up or questions concerning the 'ex', the joint past and other vitally important sensations are being raised. The most famous line men use to escape the subject of the 'ex' I have over the years found to be 'It's all behind me now; I don't want to talk about it anymore.'

Unfortunately, if not already unhappy with the existence of the 'ex' and the mysteries surrounding her, latest now the 'new' woman's defences are on 'Code Red', also known as 'the alarm bells are ringing', even if no particular reason seems to exist for any true worry. The ringing bells are intuitive soldiers, and those men not easily willing to disclose any sought after information will sooner or later end up in the line of fire. That, however, is their problem. The desire for specific information is as much in the female DNA as the desire for sex is in men's. This can easily turn into a tricky balancing act; the lack of information combined with the own suspicions usually produce lopsided conclusions and assumptions whenever the 'ex' gets a mention.

To deliver deeply sought after relief shared by countless women, a few simple *facts* deserve attention. Therefore it has firstly to be pointed out that *factually* seen, women, on the whole, sooner or later will be, are or already have been in the shoes of the 'ex' themselves – a fact representing a strange, unfortunately too often hidden or even bluntly overlooked solidarity which holds relief all in itself and therefore should enable women to develop an understanding and appreciation for peace and harmony towards each other, even if it was one of a weird nature. This little detail of actually sharing some experiences, situations and perhaps even future developments is very often forgotten, or worse, doesn't even cross women's minds.

When investigated closer this insight delivers a somewhat unexpected but intriguing view into the alleged opponent's position indeed. The simple truth might not please us, its fact, however, remains undisguised – whether we initiated the split ourselves or were forced to acknowledge it, another woman has taken our place.

Every person, female or male, has a connection to or actually is some 'ex' somewhere. Reaching a certain age automatically includes some 'ex' experiences, even if one decides to remain single for the rest of one's life – one 'ex' or more usually being responsible for this decision in the first place. Strictly speaking, relationship-life is a notoriously complex mix of tightly woven strings of 'new', 'present', 'former' and 'ex' all around and usually does not exclude anyone of averagely mad nature.

Whether the 'ex' was a long-term or only a short-term part of the own man's life, sooner or later stressful agitation is allowed to take over any possible rational thinking process concerning the ever-present 'ex', and every 'new' woman can usually sing a long and unmelodic song about this. Sometimes even brief phone calls, harmless text messages regarding the children, email reminders of mutual friends' birthdays, postcards from abroad, leftover photographs through letterboxes and invitations to gatherings of the former family drive 'new' women towards riding roughshod with themselves, ambushing any modestly attempted rational approach to not find any of this threatening. Whether it had been the 'ex' or the own man to have finished the relationship never seems to bear any importance; either way, in many 'new' women's minds 'ex's' seem to have by far too long fangs for their liking.

At times even more out of control, 'new' women's own loose imagination about the 'ex' and her potential influence on the man the two women now have in common often stretches to causes for concern. Wild worries emerge from an inner space deep down in one's soul, wondering if the own person is ever going to be a comparable part to an unknown past involving the own man and 'that other woman', even if such stir only exist superficially. Any alarm bells caused to ring louder due to men's low key flight plans don't help a blossoming mind's eye; vivid colours usually paint rainbows mostly experienced as threats rather than joy. A wild female imagination on a rampage can cause havoc well known to many.

When children are involved, the real stress starts. The bond children provide between two people will never vanish or just go away because one doesn't like this connection. Even if the 'ex' and the man share a true hatred for each other, their children remain their overlapping past way into any separated future. The sooner this is understood the more efficiently any daunting realities will become manageable. For a man of a certain age to have children once he divorces is completely widespread; after all, not many women or men plan their divorce decades prior to its happening. Having to face the existence of off-spring is both, typically and naturally inescapable.

What sounds in summery so bleak makes one wonder about the true nature of relationships and their potential danger factors when an 'ex' is involved. It's said, however, life would be dull without the spice of competition or some fruity jealousy; any conclusive thought regarding this philosophy is gladly left to the individual reader, of course. One question, however, remains uncontested – is there any hope for a less stressful life with 'new', 'present', 'former' and 'ex' mixing ruthlessly and seemingly unavoidably?

As always, the answer is simple – *yes,* and the solution to the whole 'ex'-business problem is embarrassingly undemanding, too, which makes this chapter one of the shorter ones in this little book of freedom, duly in absence of any necessity to stretch simple but effective advice over dozens and dozens of pages.

It couldn't be any easier; and this advice is for many a reason to question my sanity. Rest assured, countless women I have met whose lives were overpoweringly influenced, or so they thought, by the partner's ex could now confirm my sanity, and my common sense.

How easy? This easy – by simply bearing in mind just how many women are *virtually* in the same boat, with one sitting on portside, the other sitting on starboard side, one would love to hope this unfussy realisation delivers a tool to even out any mutually walked paths. Women everywhere, absolutely everywhere, are 'ex-women' of some sort – to remind ourselves occasionally of this tiny but often missed detail might convey a whole new and well deserved calm to this seemingly endless, too often frustrating and usually pointless friction.

Looking at it from this female-connection point of view might open up a new sight of both, previously unexpected and relieving qualities. This believed to be insane and ever so brief advice many women I have worked with found to be delivering a truly unforeseen liberation and a new, strange communal understanding; being in this unscheduled boat together, all of a sudden any overlapping life seems less taxing. The need to take the wind out of each other's sails seems now pointless, as both sides require sturdy sails to conquer the oceans.

This shared understanding and healthy give-and-take approach I have found to open doors some women on either side never expected to find moving at all. Accepting to be the 'new' woman and therefore accepting the 'ex' *and vice versa* works very well if both parties every now and then remind themselves of the possibility of tables suddenly turning without warning. *No relationship is perfect;* women and men everywhere share similar break-up stories and experiences, a thousand-fold. Things can move quite quickly when they turn sour – before many even know it they are becoming the 'ex', mostly involuntarily.

The effortless advice to show compassion with a fellow female being in similarly experienced situations I have found to be working best, despite its weird nature, and is, as predicted, short, sweet and surprising. Allowing a bit of sympathy to grow both ways truly can work wonders, and to put oneself in 'her' shoes should enable any sceptic to see the opposite side of the picture. This liberating comprehension in place, a new solidarity can evolve making everybody's life involved lots easier. One might *think* the 'ex' is a 'wicked witch', but if one looks more closely, 'harmless broom' is more likely to hit a more accurate description.

Whatever any ex with the 'factor' might have done to trigger one's anger, it's worth looking into it from a different perspective. To only ever assume utter mischief or menace to be the motive behind an action might turn out to be a plain incomprehension. Insecurities and even simple self-defence mechanisms are set off on *both* sides, more often than anticipated.

For *one* woman, from either side, to make the important first step is all it actually takes. To reach out a hand of tolerance truly works wonders; I've seen it countless times – even 'ex's' are only humans, and what one would certainly appreciate to have recognised once in the same shoes should be applied both ways.

Being a woman isn't easy. Being an 'ex' isn't easy. Being a 'new' woman isn't easy, either. Being a man is probably bad luck. Making an effort to remember all of these little wisdoms might perhaps grant life a chance to be less complicated.

It's true; nobody needs to fight at all, and the ex – factor might hold a few surprisingly positive solidarities in stock.

The next move is up to you.

'My grandmother believes I am mentally disturbed
because I chose to be single.
Being mad never felt better.'

Rachel

Being single – bad luck or great privilege?

When I first met Rachel she came to seek illumination
about the possible reasons why all men she's ever
dated were boring and dull, arrogant and obnoxious,
overflowing with self-importance and urging to
dominate or gay and married. All her relationships,
however long or short they had been and in spite of
all good intentions from her side, seemed to end in
disaster – regularly.

With the exception of wanting children, the usual
cravings and urges, itches and yearnings normally
associated with being in a relationship for so many,
like receiving Valentine's Day cards, experiencing
mini-breaks away together, cooking in unison, eating
out, eating in and eating each other, despite her
countless failed attempts were as appealing to Rachel
as ever. Then in her early thirties, the thought of
wandering through this, in her views, at times
revolting life on her own frightened her, frequently
had her experience nightmarish visions of her own
mother chasing her with baby nappies and made her

long for a male partner as much as the next person facing similar impulses.

Her endeavours stretched from an unfastened liaison with a divorced man twice her age, treating her like a shiny trophy won for outstanding sportsmanship in whatever associated discipline, to a married man experimenting with his talents to lie and deceive, practised on Rachel as much as on his wife, only lots later to be identified to involve a third woman, to a wonderfully sensitive, truly sweet and considerate young fellow discovering during lovemaking to her that he's gay. Other encounters included a computer geek in love with his mother; a recently divorced father of two, unhealthily in love with his children; a sports freak in love with himself and a lawyer in love with Justice.

Her most recently conducted experiment attempting to find a little happiness with a man saw her going to great lengths, desperately trying to use all her bad experiences to make this new relationship, a relationship looking rather promising, work beyond the initial phase of newly being in love. Unfortunately, things took a turn for the wrong on a magnitude even unknown to Rachel, despite her vast experiences of matters ultimately turning sour.

At first not suspecting anything out of the ordinary, by now Rachel was an expert in granting various types of male personalities various types of freedoms for various types of quirks, she found out rather unexpectedly that her latest boyfriend, a good looking banker of appropriate age and matching sexual direction, unmarried, with no children and no further ties, with independent financial means, a passion for cooking, travelling and curious entertainment and an apt amount of time for her, had a very unusual, very unfunny and rather devastating sense of humour. Although not prude or limited by any lack of imagination, his craze was too much even for an open-minded girl like herself.

It happened on a bus to work one morning. A group of youngsters with electronic internet access devices looked Rachel up and down as she stood holding on to a rail; they were grinning childishly, making rude and obnoxious remarks about her, barely able to contain themselves. When leaving the bus, the group shouted obscene atrocities in her direction, making fellow passengers' heads turn towards her. It happened so fast, she had difficulties taking it all in, and when she got off the bus just moments after the youngsters matters became worse.

There she was – in the nude, only her arms and her hands covering her modesties, stretching out on a red carpet on the floor of her boyfriend's living room, now depicted on a 360 square foot poster, dangling down the highest building of this corner of downtown. Her face was perfectly recognisable, and she remembers him taking this photograph well. Only about a week ago he had suggested to make her the star of an intimate photo shoot; it had felt harmless to her. In amazement she stared at herself, not sure whether she was in a nightmare or the production to a seedy movie. There was a message on the poster. Simple, ridiculous and cheap – 'My pleaser of the month'. When a few work colleagues of hers walked by all she wanted to do is to die.

According the some male colleagues awaiting her at her desk she was also to be admired on some dubious website. Rachel didn't have to watch the clip herself; her amused colleagues filled her in on all relevant details. She vaguely remembered her alleged boyfriend fiddling with his camera; now she realised he had filmed her as well.

With trance-like movements, a silent Rachel packed a few things and bits and bobs together and left. She was too shocked to even contemplate offering any explanation to her amused colleagues and her fairly traumatised boss; instinctively she felt it was too late for any facts supporting her innocence and outlining her to be the victim in this game whose rules she failed to obey.

Rachel took a taxi to his office. The mind-blowing reality surrounding her paralysed her movements, yet she knew she had no choice. His female, nervous assistant told her he was tight up in a meeting, that he couldn't possibly be disturbed and looked rather unnerved and close to fainting when Rachel turned on the spot, leaving his office and assertively walked down the hall to the conference room she knew he could be found. On her way, she grabbed a huge Blackforest Gateau cake, obviously intended for some sort of celebration in one of the adjacent offices. Luck had it the celebrations hadn't started yet.

When Rachel entered the conference room without knocking and with the massive cake in her right hand, some brief reminiscing moments flashed through her aching brain; the few weeks they had had together indeed had started out to be different, to be promising, to lead perhaps to a future. After all the trouble with unsuitable men she had encountered before, he had seemed to be a God-sent angel fulfilling all hopes for deliverance. Although already amply acquainted with feeling like an idiot most of the time, this man had managed to make her feel much worse. He had managed to make her feel a previously unknown density of humiliation, vulnerability and embarrassment, literally of epic proportions; even sleeping with a gay specimen while being informed about his sexual orientation seemed rather entertaining compared to the exposure this devil-like creature had forced upon her.

He chaired what seemed to be a critical business get-together; the room was full of important looking women and men. In his expensive suit, perfect tie and matching hand-made shirt, his custom-made shoes and cufflinks and his watch as expensive as the deposit on her flat had been, he looked convincing, serious yet accessible, competent, informed, in control and concentrated. His white teeth, manicured fingers and flawless hair completed the image seamlessly. Rachel, however, could now see beyond the make-belief.

She knew, not even a new direction of male evolution would ever let his deranged 'sense of humour' and perverted taste for fun shine through this picture perfect sight. Trying to convince everybody or anybody about her having been fooled into this morning's breaking news, discovered by half of the City, or even trying to prove his initiative and involvement would be a pointless venture and serious waste of her time. Reminding herself of her literally stripped down soul, Rachel took a deep breath, stared at him and focussed. He saw her, but he wasn't prepared. What happened next stunned even him and shook his control.

With a precision that surprised Rachel she planted the cake straight into his face. Too astonished to react he didn't even attempt to get a word out of his gateau decorated mouth. Picking a cherry which had landed on his forehead, Rachel turned around and left, on her way out enjoying the bittersweet taste of the red fruit bursting on her tongue.

Mr. Indecent was her last ever relationship with a male of the human race. Trying to convince her about him being an unusual case even within the male community proved to be a waste of effort.

Her perception of life itself changed. All previously felt needs and desires for a togetherness celebrating a harmony of mutual understandings enclosed in a relationship vanished. Men, on the whole, have lost their appeal beyond first assumptions. The idea of ever being silly enough to expose any feelings or weaknesses, preferences or opinions, views, beliefs or thoughts towards a man again, let alone share her body, made her want to crush her own head with a hammer. Rational suggestions of giving it time and allowing perhaps to heal her bruised soul only ever found deaf ears. Rachel had made up her mind. No more men for her, ever.

After having to face her superiors at work, an environment not very amused with any what is considered to be inapt behaviour, and walking by giggling immature male colleagues on the way, she had handed in her notice and decided it was time for a long break. Never having had a lifestyle beyond her financial means had enabled her to put a bit of money aside, month by month; in a desperate time of jobless and lifeless desolation it now came in handy.

From searching online herself, she had learnt the clip featuring her would be accessible for what seemed forever. The poster had remained hanging for a full week; disguised with a wig, sunglasses and wearing an old tracksuit she regularly went to have a look at the monstrosity that had cost her a much loved job, a steady financial income and the last bit of her self-esteem. Finally, after the seven longest days of her life it was replaced by a 360 square foot marriage proposal; one David was asking one Cindy to marry him on Maui, Hawai'i.

She avoided any contact with friends and family; due to too many misunderstandings and quarrels her family, she was sure, would not offer any perhaps appreciated support. Friends were contacting her mainly to make fun of her, forcing her to scratch a few always suspected to be fools off her Christmas card list. She knew, fighting this insane battle would not receive any relief from within the parameters of these two categories of humans.

The motives behind Mr. Indecent's deed to expose her to thousands and thousands of people were and remained a mystery. After many sleepless nights Rachel concluded a well hidden, appalling and very sick sense of decency with sadistic tendencies must have driven him to this act. She tortured her brain for days, wondering if she had to take any blame for some accidental wrongdoing, having caused him to release this true inner self; she even wondered if she had deserved this sort of shock therapy. Nothing of such nature emerged from her memory though, no matter how hard she searched for it.

Near breaking point every time a man stared at her with an overflowing and unusual interest, she phoned me after another of these encounters and told me the time for a change of wallpaper had come. Greece was waiting, a self-catering place on the most remote island she could find on the internet was booked and she desperately prayed for the island not to have too many laptops or indeed any remote internet access places.

I sensed her attitude had changed truly irrevocably and this new way to see life was to stay with her permanently. Not only had Rachel made her peace accepting her life to be man and relationship-free from now on, being such a lovely young woman, and to a certain extent even of already strong nature despite her youth, I knew she'd recover from this most

foul ordeals she had been put through. All it took now
was time.

Her fundamentally new mind-set was confirmed in a
letter she had sent me from her trip of soul-searching
and revival in Greece. After all she's been through
I was relieved and pleased to read about her upturn.
This letter, rather liberating and uplifting, I'd like to
share. As before in Emily's diary featuring in 'Affairs',
to serve authenticity, once more the wording remains
unchanged.

Greece, on some unpronounceable island
September 11th

Dearest Maren,
Here I am, in sunny Greece; two weeks of possibly
three more to come are already gone, and I'm pleased
to say that my recent – and last! – encounter is slowly
but surely moving from giving me nightmares to
forming the grounds for a new and lots brighter
outlook. It's amazing what sun, sand and sea far away
from it all can do for an entangled soul.

My ordeal, I think it's fair to call it that, made me
realise you can ache in places you didn't know existed
inside of you, and the journey to this stage so far was
a rather profound experience – and I don't mean the
low cost airline I had chosen to fly me here, although
that was quite a happening, too. Cattle on the way to
the abattoir travel in more style, I reckon.

Joke aside, I'm having a great time – I can't believe
I've been here two weeks already. My soul-searching

is working extremely well; I recall my own failures with various men on an hourly basis, I don't shy away from the mess they have left in my head and I take good looks around me, all the time. The news this practice reveals is overpowering, but good.

I literally look all around me all the time these days, and all I seem to see is disaster. Everywhere, absolutely everywhere I see women suffering from being in so-called relationships, allowing unhealthy compromise to take over and to be limited beyond belief. I can't but wonder, but do these women actually know any of this? I somehow doubt it; being female seems to have blindness strike on more than one occasion – I'm the best example for blind stupidity. Don't be shy, say yes! I can picture your grin. I know I am. It took me to fall very low in order to see again.

Out for dinner last night I saw a woman with a bloke at the table next to me, I went to a lovely little restaurant down by the beach, and I could feel her struggle with him ogling other women up and down. Not just a harmless, brief glance of admiration, an outright up and down scan of the female anatomy was being conducted by him; various women received this treatment, with his, I assume girlfriend, feeling every single of the guy's gazes.

She tried to have a conversation with him, but after a while gave up as it seemed pointless – his attention wouldn't shift. The anguish in her body language felt familiar to my own previous stiffness – how many times have I been in a similar position? I lost count...

but I do remember feeling stupid, inappropriate
and lonely every time the man of the moment felt
shamelessly free to have his eyes wonder endlessly,
not embarrassed to even comment on several occasions
on breast shapes and whether small pointy ones are
nicer than big round ones. When in a relationship,
I concluded, this sort of behaviour is not on; when
women and men are just friends, it doesn't bother me
the slightest. I guess inner freedom literally frees one
from this pressure.

This morning, in a little breakfast bar near the hotel,
a similar limitation happened again, like other
mornings before; but only today it really clicked
when I witnessed it. Another couple, and since there
aren't many people here you get to know people's
behavioural patterns, sat not far away from me and
although this time the male creature wouldn't stare at
women, he would boss his own girl around as if she
were a little kid. He didn't even do it in a nasty way,
just subtle little hints like 'I suggest not having more
cream cheese, darling, you know how fattening it is'
or 'do you think another coffee will do your IBS any
good?' or 'let's go, the sun's best now, I want to take
those shots' – and he grabbed her, forcing her to leave
her unfinished roll with thinly spread cream cheese
behind.

I couldn't believe it! I sensed her desire to behead
him, yet she did nothing about him treating her like a
child, or worse!, a little puppy. I remember my own
moments of having been in such a situation – you hold
on, you hope things will get better, you don't fight,

you don't quarrel, you don't think, it doesn't occur to you that the guy might be wrong, in short – <u>you let it happen</u>. I wish more women would wake up like I'm doing on this trip – and never fall asleep again!

Here's another one – the other day I witnessed yet another female limitation – this time it concerned a gorgeous, truly beautiful woman, probably my age, with a body a girl like me can only dream about, trying to catch her breath after what looked like a heated march down from the hotel. She had a look on her face indicating to me she had just escaped a man. She had arrived alone with a towel and beach bag and settled in the hot sand not far away from me. I sensed she was very close to crying, but she held back the tears somehow; I wondered why, but everything about her felt like agony. I couldn't help but stare at her; too much did she remind me of my own very disastrous, to say the least, experiences with men, only without the beauty, of course.

When her bloke arrived about twenty minutes later their problem became obvious at once – he was the jealous kind of guy. Despite it being forty-two degrees Celsius in the shade and probably one thousand degrees in the blazing sun he insisted she'd hide in a long oversized t-shirt he'd thrown at her, with sleeves down to the elbows, and to make matters worse, which had a print reading 'Been there, done it, got this t-shirt'. I felt very sorry for her.

Yet, and yet again like the other two women before, she didn't really object, didn't really challenge him verbally. She just had this look on her face; to me, it spoke 'anguish' out loud, just as I have done so many times… A little while later, when it simply was too hot to sit in a t-shirt and very much to the horror of her boyfriend she took off the useless piece of clothing and walked, no, floated into the sea. I bet she toyed with the idea of never coming back out again… When she eventually emerged, all men in the near vicinity ogled her Bo Derek body up and down, as she truly and honestly looked amazing. The refreshing water of the sea must have not just refreshed her body, but her mind, too – she argued with him, verbally. I had already began to feel hope, but then she gave in again, put on the t-shirt and left. He followed her shouting some ridiculous accusations too irrelevant to repeat. It was the last I have seen of them.

Maren, I'm telling you, all these stories around me, and these were only a small cross section of what you can see when one's here for weeks at a time, made me think. Other observations include women being the 'new' woman in a father's life, the 'new' family spending their first – and probably last – vacation together and the agony these women go through, yet you have to admire them for their good faith and hope and willpower to not drown any kids; others relate to women having to put up with notorious drunks at any time of day festering over the loss of an ex-girlfriend; mothers not receiving any help with the children from the fathers whatsoever, because they are too busy watching TV in a pub or watching women on the beach or women who realise while away for a week or two that 24/7 with the man of the moment can only and inevitably lead to a break-up as soon as they are back home. Apart from fellow single ladies, not one woman around me seems to be happy in her relationship. No one! Where are the happy ladies – on Hawai'i?

I befriended a couple of single ladies here, who have co-incidentally been through similar nightmares themselves, although they didn't have to explain to their mothers why they suddenly quit a job they love. Greece, this island especially, must be a magnet for devastated female egos on the mend. Or perhaps it's so suitable because it's far away from the real world.

It makes me wonder, all of this. It underlined, put in italic and made all thoughts in my broken head go bold, all at the same time – no more men for me, _ever_! Being a single is _the_ way to go for me from now on; if I had been in any doubt about it before, now I'm sure. God, I cannot express just how lucky I feel to have finally understood the nature of it! And what a relief! I never have to put up with any shit anymore, ever! This revelation is illumination, liberation and independence all in one throw; certainly the best thing that has ever happened to me. It's perhaps sad it took me so long to realise my position in the whole relationship rat race, but the penny has now dropped, finally dropped.

From now on I can do exactly what I want, when I want it and how I want it. I can eat whatever I want without anybody ever feeling the need to express concern for my hip size; I can drink whatever I want without anybody ever criticising me for it; I can go to places I choose, stay out for as long as I want to

without having to worry about having raised
suspicions or causing idiotic jealousies. And I can
watch on TV whatever I want without a male
distracting me with his version of telly fun – watching
twenty channels all at the same time. When I watch a
DVD I don't have to worry about his eyes wonder to
the wrong subject on the screen. Not having to ever
worry again about what his ex might try to still
contact him is another great relief. I certainly had my
fair share of those blunders… Last but not least I love
the thought of being able to live my quirks happily;
nobody will ever judge me about my loving little
specialities anymore. Never having to explain, or
worse, having to defend myself is the best of all.

Gosh, this feels so good! I know you said to me my
last experience was an extreme one, but I don't care
just how many good guys might be out there – I'm
sure there are plenty of women who are more than
happy to entertain these men. Me, however, I'm not.

In three short words – I am free!

I can also – finally – kiss the while lovemaking
business goodbye – no more of those sorrows for me!
It had its good elements; I admit that, but it also has
no irreplaceable value, not for me. Mind you, saying
that, I let you in, my little secret, I had some great sex
the other night, with a very willing victim called…
you know what, I've forgotten his name – that
can only mean I'm on the mend! I didn't want Mr.
Indecent to have been my last man, it's as simple as
that. The district's water supplier's good looking son

didn't protest – why would he? Sex without strings attached works for him on a daily basis, very much to the delight of the local pharmacist. It was a one-off, on my terms and conditions, and I'm pleased to announce that my self-respect is on the way back in; it had been off course for a very long time.

No more agenda, other than my own, and work, once I have a job again, but that's fine. I don't mind work commitments. No more Christmas or New Year's with people I either don't know or don't like, just because the man of the moment insisted we visit his aunt. The list of things I did do but didn't really want to do is long... but whom am I telling, you know them all.

Why did I never protest? Until now I never really asked myself that question, not even when we met, you and me, I mean. I've always thought it must all be my fault when things went wrong in my relationships. It's beyond me now and shivers me with horror why and just how much I accepted second best for such a long time – how desperate are women??? How desperate was I to put up with insincere, deceiving, perverse, immature, boyish, selfish, arrogant, sex-obsessed, drunk, workaholic, unfaithful specimen?

The answer is simple: I didn't know I wanted to be single. Now I do. Besides, my own behaviour hasn't always been saint-like. I have lied to men to get better deals or have lied about being out with a girlfriend while, in fact, I had been out with a male colleague. Just a colleague indeed, however, I lied about my friendship with him because I wanted to avoid

questions about it. Jealousy is like salt in a soup –
too little makes it blunt, too much spoils it. I realise
nobody is perfect, least of all me, but at times I've
turned it into an art form to pick truly unsuitable,
relationship-unsuitable men. Moreover, another
positive and not to be underestimated side effect is the
valuable realisation of never having to lie or to hurt
others, well, men, anymore either. This deal works
both ways, a thought I quite indulge in.

Maren, I close this long letter now; the finally cooling
down summer night's air is waiting for me to breathe
it – the first time in a long time the air around me feels
pollution free.

I catch you when I'm back home – single, but happy.
Love,
Rachel

When Rachel returned she was transformed, truly
transformed. She moved out of her flat and into a
little, even cheaper house on the outskirts of the city,
changed all her phone numbers, even her email
address. Her address book shrank to the bare
minimum of true friends, amazingly all of them old
friends from the past she had neglected during her
many years of being in wrong relationships. Now
happier than ever, she revived a few precious
friendships and built herself an entirely fresh, very
carefully chosen social circle. Contrary to what one
could expect her female friends weren't all single, far
from it. Two or three were in relationships, even

married with children, but Rachel never felt tempted to fill others in on her illuminations of a woman's one and true existence to be most successful when being single; she had decided to leave this secret for every woman to find out for herself.

The new job she found was more than good for her ego. Her newly acquainted self-confidence made her stand out from the crowd of applicants; it took her no time at all to conquer her new professional quest and she invested all her independence into her daytime. At night, when alone but not lonely, she celebrated freedom the way it's described in her book. Evenings out with old new friends, sleeping as long as she wanted at weekends and throwing dinner parties for caring fellow human beings every now and then.

Quite often, she also decided to simply stay at home. The work around her new house filled her with previously unknown satisfaction, something she never thought she'd enjoy. Nightmares involving strange men vanished. What Rachel called her 'true contentment' had taken over her inner self.

Men she made stay out of her life – for good, as she would say. Neither temptations of sexy looking bums nor magic spells spoken over her by her grandmother changed her mind. One might think she turned into an anti-man woman, but she didn't. A few of her friends are male, even are close friends. Rachel wasn't anti-men, she was anti-relationship; she was now complete in herself as a woman of substance.

Rachel is only one example of many I have met over the years. The idea of living relationship-free and therefore hassle-free is tempting and represented the only way for most women I worked with once they made up their minds to live and breathe this liberating lifestyle. However, many have also enquired about a re-assurance that this way of living was neither a crime nor verification for being relationship-suckers. After establishing this successfully, their inner independence grew to even greater proportions and as in chapters before, efficient advice doesn't have to be long and complicated to be clear and effective.

The number of women longing for liberation from limiting, unhealthy compromises stemming from the second best relationship they find themselves in is so vast, the many various examples I could offer would fill a whole book; no surprise to anybody ever feeling the desire to break free.

Spinsterhood is *not* the worst thing you can choose or have chosen to embark on; being single is a lifestyle choice like choosing to live child-free or sex-free, diet-free or family-free. It's very much down to the individual, *without any wrong or right,* to which extent this personal freedom is being fulfilled. As far as living free from the commitment of a relationship is concerned, it's neither a testament for one's ability to commit to a partner nor a death row sentence. Millions of women the world over, and men for that matter of fact, enjoy a singleton life full of personal freedom they find would otherwise be vanishing or practically be non-existing when in a relationship.

This perception is private; no further reasons need to be found.

The choice to choose is a fundamental right for every person, female or male. Many families find it a worry when their female members seem to remain single with progressing age, wondering about the reasons and trying the best they can to find cures – or men. When male members remain single, they are admired for their persisting freedom-seeking technologies; an unfair myth that needs to be send back to the Dark Ages in countless women's eyes.

If Rachel was any guide, one could of course argue she's been very unlucky many times over and with time she might find the right man. Of course this is true; however, it will only ever be of any interest to any woman still on the quest to seek happiness from a union. Rachel has not only cancelled all her previous emotions and desires linked to relationships, she's re-arranged her views, and after experimenting with her inner vision of her life to come she had decided to withdraw herself from the man race. A move entirely individual, but legitimate nonetheless.

Being single is neither wrong nor right just like being in a relationship isn't wrong or right. *It's personal*; it's a lifestyle choice, not more, not less. The women I have worked with all had in common that they worried at one point or another about the 'wrongs' and 'rights' the singleton existence bears in their own eyes, but especially in the eyes of others, mostly when family get involved. Self-doubts emerged every time a family member, usually of female nature, felt free to criticise the spinster status. Especially in older generations the idea of remaining single equals hopelessness and tragedy, being unwanted and uncared for. Another myth many of my single ladies are only too happy to correct.

It's very simple, brief and uncomplicated – if the thought of ever being in a relationship is causing you to fear panic attacks, avoid these internally felt tie-downs with pride. You're making the right decision. This world is still somewhat a free place, having to justify individual decisions shouldn't have to occur. The chapter about 'self-acceptance' goes deeper into the nature of individual verdicts of this and many other subjects – it might be a good idea to have a back-up.

If you have always been a single, you will know why – so enjoy it. In case you still feel haunted by outside influences, the chapter about 'family' introduces some valuable aid about how to, for instance, handle family members with different approaches to your own more easily. Rachel's grandmother still hopes for her grandchild to agree to therapy; yet something tells me Rachel will refuse, respectfully.

Many singles, either after newly discovering this particular freedom or after years of leading a single life, came to seek advice on how to emotionally manage the expectations of others or indeed their own peculiar feeling and suspicion that being single was indeed the formerly unknown personal preference.

The desired re-assurance that being alone was not a crime was an all too known emotional fear.

Spinster, single, unattached, free or bachelorette – whatever name you give it, it's not a crime. It's deliverance for many, and a lifestyle filling countless women who have not found an inner courage to break free just yet with jealousy. A jealousy usually replaced with illumination, however, as soon as they break free.

Being single – bad luck or great privilege?

You choose.

**'My childhood was plain madness;
studying psychology was the logical consequence.'**

Maren

Your childhood – the most pleasant time of your life?

Quite frankly, I don't think so. Personally, I'd rather live on a somewhat deserted and oxygen deprived planet in a space suit and surrounded only by a few green aliens for the rest of my life, if I had to, before I'd go back to childhood, let alone puberty again.

Endless rubbing against siblings; struggling for the sought after attention of adults; cheating to get the best of whatever deal; lying about anything and everything, especially about money; constantly fighting to be heard or to be taken seriously, and of course making a complete idiot of oneself when first trying to copy Farah Fawcett's hairstyle – no, thanks, not for me or for most of the women I met over the years whenever the subject of childhood came up and what 'childhood' can represent if one had been an unlucky youngster.

Crushing jealousy, one of many nasty factors while being an adolescent, especially in early puberty, certainly was no joy – but being jealous of everybody and everything was customary. Jealous of the school's

favourite classmate because she had longer legs;
jealous of the own sister because she was Grandma's
favourite; jealous of the girl next door because she
managed, despite her weird Goth outfit and matching
make-up, to pull the best looking eighteen year old
boy in the neighbourhood, who, now topping the
envy, was the proud owner of a car. A nearly
decomposed VW Golf, but a car, nonetheless.

To make matters worse, one day rather unexpectedly,
the unpleasant business of periods had to be dealt
with. For a young girl not knowing much about it,
it represented quite a challenge at first, and when
I was little this wasn't a subject one normally
discussed with anybody other than perhaps a
girlfriend at school or a female sports coach. Even
mothers didn't at large prepare their daughters to
see to such events.

The past – often too present
Childhood is obviously a part of our lives nothing
can be changed about, as much as of course pretty
much anything in our past is, in fact, exactly that – *the
past*. And as much as the past might have moments
of fading from our memory, our childhood is a
compressed compartment of that past, which even if
roughly forgotten, subconsciously remains in some
remote corner of our heads. When those memories
reflect bad experiences, we can be in trouble.

What is the most pleasant memory of your childhood?
Was it Christmas, with all the decorations, the lights,
the sweeties and, of course, the presents? Or was it

perhaps your grandmother with her homemade biscuits and her warm welcoming smile which revive sweet memories? Perhaps having been popular with the teachers back in school puts a smile on your face?

Birthdays, especially your own, your pet cat or school days out – if thinking back to your childhood triggers warm and comforting giggles in your soul and doesn't cause a panic attack then consider yourself lucky.

Not so lucky are those women who have found themselves in various wonky situations in their childhood and although while a child entirely beyond their control, suffered from daunting consequences, worrying memories, even if some of them were fading, and at times overwhelmingly dominant influences these circumstances can characterise.

The list of possible askew situations is long. There are countless scenarios which unfortunately can victimise a woman's adulthood due to unaddressed issues, which makes living with them a real challenge. This can reach the point of many women's dreams at night turning into truly vicious nightmares; waking up sweating and shaking, plagued by disorientation, becomes a re-occurring theme. Lots of women only remember some bizarre reverie about unpleasant images and if at all, only a few distorted details can be recalled. In my case, I had been haunted by cotton balls with extended arms and large faces for a very long time.

A touch of autobiography – a brief case study

I was very young, only six years of age, when my father died. The memory of the fuss everybody put me through because of this dreadful fact discomforted me for years to come. If I could have had it my way, although having been heart-broken and feeling very sorry for my mother, I would have just wanted to play with my toy cars, hiding in some place I considered safe. However, the attention I became exposed to was inescapable; everyone wanted a piece of the poor, young, now fatherless girl, so my desired approach to grief didn't seem likely to stand a chance. Having been spoiled with attention before, until that day, however, I had not the faintest idea just how much pity can pour towards one single person.

Although it was widely assumed I was too young to fully realise what had happened to my father, I understood the meaning of death well. He had been very sick for many months, and my mother had excessively prepared me for this consequence to eventually be undeniable. In spite of its demoralising implication and overpowering sadness, never being able to see him again I had learnt to accept long before his death was looming. After all, I had my mother to clasp to tightly.

Metaphorically wrapping me into cotton wool for months to come, my family's approach of handling the heartbreaking loss of my father had unpleasant side effects. The sense of embarrassment was overwhelming and hart to flee from. Many trivial situations have triggered emotions of this tremendous awkwardness whenever the subject of 'death' came up, either innocently on TV or accidentally during family reminiscing.

While widely agreed that expressed fuss usually generates feelings of wellbeing and support, love and understanding, in my situation it was more a case of nightmarish occurrences of weird mountains of cotton balls and huge faces gazing over me. At one point it became so absurd the cotton balls grew arms and had a go at grabbing me, waking me fearing for my safety. It was peculiar, to say the least.

It's strange how life now and then exposes its eccentric ways. It seemed it wouldn't want to unchain me any time soon and it appeared that co-incidences are rarely anything other than a pompous life itself playing nasty tricks on people or giving them a nice, or in my case obliterate, surprise – my mother died of cancer only seventeen months after my father had passed away. While until then the devastatingly sad emotions of having lost my father were somewhat contained by the support my mother had unconditionally spoiled me with, now entirely on my own the real troubles began. I remember the day the news about my mum's death reached me. It was a very cold January morning, a Sunday morning, and I remember wonderfully blue and clear skies. My mother was in hospital in a town half an hour drive away and I was supposed to see her that day as usual. Sunday was mum-visiting-day, something I remember looking forward to all week. During my mother's hospital stays I used to stay with a friend of the family; a dear elderly lady, and she had always taken very good care of me.

The youngest of five siblings, all other children long grown up, my elder sister broke the news to me that morning. I found her in tears at the family home, the house in which my father had died and my mother and I had created a very intimate and safe bubble of grief for us. The tables had turned once more; grief was to be extended, now including the bereavement of my mother.

Within a few hours the whole family, all my siblings, their spouses and their very young children – I was only seven years of age, but was already an auntie to two nieces and one nephew – all aunts and uncles and their children and also all neighbours and their offspring arrived at the house. Like the elders in a rural tribe the adults huddled to discuss my future.

Adapting to the thought of Mum being gone was tough. Strangely surreal emotions surrounded me for the next part of a journey which to describe aptly I lack adequate words. The outlook was blurred, and the finally befriended nightmarish cotton balls with stingy arms turned nasty once again and returned mercilessly to my night-time. This time, I was certain, they would stay hostile for lots longer.

My life had changed for good. The mere realisation of this unbelievable fact had catapulted me into a gloomed existence of sorrow and disbelief. Countless mornings followed this fateful Sunday awakening, and hoping all this murk was only an overhanging shadow of a night just gone dictated my days. Losing my father had been hard-hitting. Losing my mother was a different matter altogether.

A few months later, in the meantime I had stayed with the caring and adorable old lady as before, a Judge decided about my mid-term future. I moved in with my eldest sister and her family; sister, brother-in-law and niece became my new immediate family and life as I knew it was now officially an overwhelmingly far away memory.

Although very young when facing the loss of Mum – any higher Architect knows I struggled with acceptance, bathing in astonishment about such unfairness happening, grieving and fighting with an indescribable sore state of mind – and given the absence of having a choice, eventually I coped. Perhaps she had a premonition, but in hindsight my mother had somewhat prepared me already during her lifetime for herself becoming a fatality of cancer's callous and vicious powers. Her mammoth strength dealing with her husband's death shone through in my memories and made me deal, however humbly, with the third death experience of my ever so juvenile life; my grandmother had died in our family house right before my eyes when I was only four, a death in retrospective nowhere near as impacting as the deaths of my parents.

In spite of muddling through, even if only modestly, the cotton balls stayed for what seemed never-ending years; pitilessly they visited during the hours of darkness, grew smaller one night, only to grow bigger the next. In addition to my nightly intimidating visitors the embarrassment following the fussing over my person when I had entered an epoch of bewildering tragedy consequently left me ashamed every time the subject of the early deaths of my parents, and grandmother, caused a compassion attack within the souls of family, friends, neighbours or teachers, and for the longest time I feared this might stand in the way of a 'normal' development, whatever 'normal' might mean. Then, one day, something changed.

I was fourteen years old when in a moment of illumination, sentimentally experienced while visiting my parents' grave, I realised that my life will always be driven by my early childhood years and the events associated with it. An impact as huge as losing one's parents at such fragile age clearly had to have some lasting affect into adulthood. Luckily, only a day later I also discovered these events didn't automatically have to be destructive; the first time since my mother's death I felt what could be described as blessed, also stronger than ever before; it certainly marked the arrival of a new, different and exhilarating era in a confused teenage girl's life.

That day, when my best girlfriend hadn't turned up at school because her mother had suddenly died, a modest, however, very valid 'click' inside me confirmed the change within taking place. While not being able to fully comprehend at the time, I had the faint suspicion that my own confrontation with loss and grief all of a sudden became a handy gift – a manifestation until then I was convinced was impossible to portrait. The heavy shadow hanging over me broke up, a very strange shiny enlightenment replaced it a bit at the time and the irresistible urge to hold up my best friend's shaken spirit emerged. The time to *accept* what I cannot change, ignoring all despair, had come – my agony turned into virtue.

One might think it's a too simple an example to stand a valid comparison to meaningful conversions from 'bad' into 'good'. However, the most effective and positive changes usually take place on formally unknown grounds, at times even seemingly minimal ones. A tiny new understanding and an unassuming elucidation is all it sometimes takes. Paired with the willingness to experiment with an open awareness it supports new ways beyond mind's eye. In my case, the realisation of my experiences to be of any positive use and even value strengthened my outlook on life to come.

Living within my immediate family, until then rather bothersome and never-endingly maddening, became manageable; concentrating on getting through puberty without any major emotional damage became an important hub, and counting the years, months, weeks and days until my eighteenth birthday kept me focussed and motivated. Growing stronger ever day, nights filled with fears of unfairness, insufficient choices, cruel ruthlessness and tremendous grief eased. Soon the domineering cotton balls faded into distant memory. Adulthood, I concluded, could only turn out well.

Despite countless possible traumatic experiences during childhood, it is a stark and undisputable fact those events don't automatically have to cause a suffering for the rest of one's life. Not just in my meek autobiographic example, many women in similar or worse situations forced upon them in infancy have – once coming to terms with some surprisingly beneficial properties – used their past to improve their future.

While at first confused by feasible and positive effects, women I have worked with have also eventually realised that the acceptance of this rather unexpected profit was suppressed by a subconscious line of bitter thoughts being used as excuses to face an ordeal. The constant avoidance of any dire subject forced women to ignore any viable gain.

The secret ammunition proven to be invaluable in the conversion of bad childhood experiences to good adulthood know-how is the facing of any bad experiences from *one* pure factual point of view, and as perhaps predicted, this advice will at first seem too easy and too compact to be efficient, as it is easy and compact indeed – practise understanding, *true* inner comprehension that nothing resting in the past, not anything that happened can be changed whatsoever, and *confrontation* is the underrated and surprisingly effective tool to aid this poignant mental homecoming. Dozens of women can confirm that this one step programme works – it's simple, but effective.

Useful tool
Every woman chooses to employ a different utensil during the adventure exchanging horrific memories into supportive future payback, but most of the ladies

I worked with found writing down their thoughts
and emotions, worries and experiences, hatreds and
disappointments to be of great help and comfort.
These journals, might they hold fresh or already fading
memories, boast marvellous healing powers if used
correctly. Numerous women I have met struggled with
this profound verity at first; with every page filled,
however, any gruesome suffering caused by childhood
encounters eventually diminishes, and reading your
own story with a neutral pair of eyes will promote this
curing. A rising self-belief is an unexpected additional
and extraordinarily pleasant side effect caused by this
confrontation; countless women can confirm this
amazing by-product, all of them grateful for such
unanticipated expansion of the mind.

Dire, most foul occurrences

The list of 'bad' is long – sexual abuse, subject to
bullying at school or in the neighbourhood, even
bullying within the family, losing loved-ones at an
early age, losing loathed family members before
achieving emotional closure, kidnapping and near-
death experiences like drowning in summer camp's
swimming competitions, accidentally being locked in
the cellar of an old country mansion, the loss of the
most beloved toy, never having received any pocket
money or having been stuck in a school below or
above their intellectual potential, traumatising
jealously causing brain paralysis, financial poverty
and deprivation of parental support and understanding, experiencing emotional blackmail,
psychological violence and physical beatings, the too
early influences of alcohol or even drug abuse – all

this, negligence in general and more can leave any
woman bruised for life. Although not immediately
seen as a bad thing, also a too overpowering love
and a well-meant but damaging sugar-coating, a
too soft approach suppressing a child's independence
and a too frequent interference with the offspring's
opinions and views can leave scars and make having
to face the fight of life in adulthood complicated
at times.

A crusade well worth it

Even such tremendously unthinkable experience as
sexual abuse does not have to automatically traumatise
one for life. Often a surprise to most, I have met women
who have been put through unbelievably terrible
sexual torments and atrocities as children and still, with
a formally unexpected but achievable fighter's attitude,
they have recovered and led a 'normal' life, free from
haunting nightmares and limiting thoughts for a fine
tomorrow.

Whatever 'bad' in one's life represents and despite
all possible sympathy, only ever festering over what
went wrong never has and never will change neither
one's attitude nor one's ability to make good use of
the past. Only a heart-felt confrontation with any
personal list of 'bad' will help to accomplish closure
and a possibly worthy future; the acceptance of 'bad'
being part of *a past that cannot be changed* is crucial.
This advice does not suggest agreeing with 'bad' from
long-ago, far from it. It's perfectly reasonable to hate
what had gone astray; fact remains though, turning
back the clock is not an option.

Adopting the irresistibly uncomplicated 'fact' approach seems perhaps too simple, yet based on its simplicity it proves precisely to be the only effectual way to venture. Deliverance from haunting thoughts of past experiences not only is deeply desired but now stands a rational chance of becoming any suffering woman's rescue; a phenomenon widely met with surprise and greatly accepted with a sigh of relief once established.

To free yourself is the key; full-on attack to convert 'bad' into 'unfortunately not reversible' will enable you to make your life, especially your tomorrow, much stronger. Allowing your moving on to happen is an uplifting experience, strongly recommended to experiment with. Peaceful tranquillity and impressive courage, invincible self-confidence and inner calm as well as a sense of achievement all result from facing the bad time long gone.

Your tomorrow – not far to go now
Your childhood is in the past; however, the rest of your life is still ahead of you. The mere acceptance of the fact that what happened in the past can't be changed supports countless grateful women to move on.

We can't change whatever went wrong, but we *can* change how to handle it. Finding peace of mind stands a good chance if only the desire for a wonderfully uncontrollable lust and curiosity for a brighter tomorrow is allowed to grow. Not because of my own childhood experiences is this chapter close to my heart; witnessing countless women to truly turn their lives around with this simple but effective and so easily accomplishable approach held uplifting and very satisfying properties in stock, not just for myself but for all others battling similar wars.

Give your vexing childhood a chance to settle in to where it belongs – in your past. Once all is said and done, the wonderful feeling of independence will stir your heart. Accepting what cannot be changed will inspire a long longed for self-confidence – *now life's up to you.*

'Wanting to hide because it's easier
seemed a good idea at first.
It's when I stopped talking to
myself I really started to worry.'

Irene

Your comfort zone – how trapped are you?

According to my professors back in university, the
'comfort zone' is a behavioural state within which
a person usually operates in an anxiety-neutral
condition, using a limited set of behaviours to deliver
a steady level of performance, usually without a sense
of extended risk. The state of 'neutral' varies thereby
greatly from person to person; some seek solace and
comfort in never leaving their bedroom glued to a TV
screen while others at least move around the house or
extend their venturing into the garden and still find
themselves in a neutral state of anxiety. What sounds
so elaborate drives many women subconsciously
towards emotional breaking point.

The intuitive search for comfort and emotional hiding
on more than one level forces countless women into
increased isolation. The daily grind seeking avoidance
of anything representing emotional danger factors
or other risks sooner or later takes its toll. The age
of women and even girls is no indication for any
special stage of comfort zone constructing. Tensions

simmering beneath the surface can evolve as early as in teenager years and don't automatically stop with progressing age. There's no waypoint to wait for a comfort zone to simply disappear.

When either undetected or indeed untreated, comfort zones can develop from relatively harmless little cages into outright terror zones. Whatever the subject of avoidance resembles, it will grow bigger and bolder and more terrifying with every point of possible contact. The simple task of facing, for instance, some work situations which might drive a person into insecurity attacks can enhance their harmful influence to the extent of making people hide in the stationary cupboard numerous times a week.

Comfort zones also have a huge impact on indicating a person's personality as far as one's individual 'power factor' is concerned. The 'power factor' of a person very much dictates a person's personal progressing from the beginning of any career to further grounds being a persistent and distinct forward movement. Although their 'tomorrow' is an unknown, the success of 'today' is intuitively used to fuel motivation and ensures the willingness to not shy away from unfamiliar situations. Very successful business people or people commonly referred to as 'Celebrities' usually step outside their comfort zones to accomplish what they aim for – as we all know with great success. Insecure, non-daring, quiet people consciously or subconsciously, despite the desire to flee from self-made limitations and ill compromises, try to avoid this at all cost.

Conclusively, a comfort zone very much represents a state of mind; it determines the openness or stressed out up-tightness of a person's thinking process. Although it has been proven to not protect a person, the comfort zone, in many longing minds, creates an unfounded sense of security. Thus very insecure persons tend to have a far greater need for comfort zones than daring, determined, self-confident and outgoing people. The more open one's mind is the more open the particular person becomes.

The connection between insecurities of various natures and comfort zones is stark. Many women's need for self-made shelter is determined by their own visions of inadequacy in the eyes of others. They judge themselves mercilessly and act as if on death row. Their subconscious mind intuitively tries to protect from any painful exposure with a homemade comfort zone, usually expressed by hiding.

A comfort zone does not automatically represent locking oneself away at home *all* the time, but I have found this to be the most often occurring consequence to be women's answer to many troubles. Comfort zones have many faces – the opposite action to anything one can identity underlining the nature of avoidance is a comfort zone, for example only ever wearing trousers due to feeling *uncomfortable* wearing skirts is a comfort zone. On balance, it's down to self-confidence and independence again, sought by millions. *Once filled with self-confidence, comfort zones don't stand a chance to rule over a person's mind.*

Comfort zone – foe or friend in disguise?
Although widely referred to as limiting, the comfort zone also functions as an ally in battling the very same. It is indeed a paradox, as it provides a helping hand in escaping from its own nature at the same time it limits us, and works as a great reminder that facing limitations is crucial to be faced in order to break free. Your comfort zone is an alarm bell ringing vigorously; it notifies you the time for change has come.

Confused? No need, it's quite simple. The insecurities which limit many women in the first place vanish progressively and almost automatically as soon as the initial step towards the *outside* of one's comfort zone takes place. Taking the eventual absence of insecurities into consideration, the need for further comfort zones is no longer given. This undemanding first step is only the very liberating beginning; in due course to enjoy the nature of self-confidence holds the real inspiring and uplifting virtues.

Once the first step is being taken, something very interesting and rather unexpected happens – the simple knowledge and awareness of being *outside* the comfort zone will involuntarily enhance your level of concentration and focus, the functioning and the effective delivering of a task. All of a sudden the terrors of the unexpected and the visions of bad experiences from the past disappear, fruitfully forcing to change the comfort or even terror zone into a much desired performance zone.

Unleashed potential
Most amazingly, women stuck in a comfort zone are internally bursting with huge and valuable potential; countless ladies I have worked with sooner or later discovered their true capabilities and talents; there are artists hidden, and good communicators, teachers and perhaps even future Prime Ministers can be found within many.

Strictly speaking just a bad habit
It comes as a surprise to many, but being stuck in a comfort zone very much resembles a habit; a nasty, truly bad habit, in fact. It's something you have been carrying around with you like an old jumper, totally crappy but perfectly serving its purpose, the jumper of course being the lesser of the two nuisances.

Example: a brief case study - Irene
One of my best friends used to be a client of mine. When Irene and I met she was in her early forties, had a well-paid job, a personal CV revealing her fair share of failed relationships and the matching face to go with it. It became clear very quickly that she reached a point in her life where no matter which direction she turned she saw no road or track to follow and no future to look forward to. She just wanted to drop dead, stone dead. Feeling like a failure became the tenet of her life.

The first time we met Irene was a sweet picture of misery; to have neither a concept, nor an idea, nor any joy, let alone any motivation was all that occupied her brain. Hardly any other thoughts stood a chance; especially no positive view could survive in this skull filled to the rim with desolation. She couldn't pinpoint an isolated problem; she summarised that absolutely nothing in her life seemed to function, was in a million pieces, not worth her while or just plain stupid.

Although without much effort from her side a very beautiful woman, Irene came across as the very ugly duckling. It was evident she wished for a better tomorrow or indeed for deliverance from a possible tomorrow altogether. During this first session it became apparent that she had built herself a huge habit based comfort zone of avoidance around her. Too many bad experiences with men, too many challenges at work shedding her self-confidence to bits and a too demanding mother expecting grandchildren had forced her into hiding. She could easily have qualified for the 'Hermit of the Year Award'.

At work she felt very uncomfortable in almost any imaginable situation. Whether it was talking to others casually or attending business matters, Irene never felt adequately prepared, under control, let alone happy with her own performance. Everything felt like a 'hit and miss' experience to her. When confrontation being a spinster, either at work or at bi-monthly meetings with her family, wasn't escapable, she found herself justifying her views to others, edging towards sound apologies, and hating every minute of it. Instinctively she knew she'd turned into an under-confident 'people pleaser'.

The hatred of her inabilities and sensed insecurities triggered a vicious circle. The less able she felt to escape, the more uncomfortable some situations became; avoiding these situations generating emotional friction within her seemed the logical consequence. Inevitably, the loss of self-confidence hit her next. The less she interacted with people, the more her self-confidence fled. At work Irene worried people could smell her insecurities, she began to avoid any extra contact with anybody, limited her interactions to purely minuscule business related issues, and tried to avoid others as much as she could possibly dare without getting fired for hiding in the stationary cupboard. When not in the stationary cupboard, she veiled at home.

It was imperative to break the mould named 'bad habit comfort zone' she had wedged herself into. If not addressed now, Irene's emotional dilemmas would boomerang back into her face forever and as a consequence life would ebb away if not grabbed.

A bad habit - and the brain is to blame
A marvel of the human nature, the luxury of thought is said to be unique to humankind. Sadly, it also incorporates the lesser appreciated ability to come up with bewildered material to impair the thinker – turning one's misery into a bad habit and implementing many damaging ways is one of them.

Our imagination is ferocious when allowed to envision the worst of any matters possible. Being miserable is one potential problematic matter, and certainly no woman aims for it. Unhappiness and vulnerability stem from this misery; the fear of exposure, bleak weakness, intolerant irritability and brusque annoyance against oneself and the rest of the world, paired with self-pity and helplessness limit the mind even further. This emotional combat zone unavoidably leads straight into the enclosure of a comfort zone, *and your brain is the enemy awaiting you on that battlefield.*

Feeling emotionally miserable is anchored in the brain, yet the very same brain stops us from taking up a fight against this misery. It's a very strange occurrence and derives from the pathological need for familiarity. Feeling home in a certain place, driving to work a certain route, eating the same meals over and over, even holiday destinations – we naturally aim for familiar surroundings, actions and activities. They merely make us feel comfortable. The human brain works very hard to establish this comfort gained from familiarity. The connection between feeling comfortable and experiencing familiarity causes an odd event to come to pass in your brain – it triggers habitual behaviour. When it comes to misery, the logical consequence is even more peculiar. Feeling miserable 24/7 for a long period of time triggers the brain to gain familiarity and therefore comfort from this distress – *despair becomes a habit.*

These almost chemically driven reactions subconsciously cause one to constantly self-manipulate any attempt to escape the misery. Staying in the comfort zone becomes the brain's priority, and no matter to what extent logical explanation or reasoning is offered, the brain greatly ignores all efforts or even fights back aggressively; it likes feeling comfortable and it likes familiarity – if 'misery' is the subject delivering this, so be it. Very bluntly put, you are used to feeling crap; feeling bad becomes normal, this 'normal' feeling becomes familiar, this familiarity creates a habit. In even simpler words – unhappiness drives us to build a comfort zone which solely exists due to the *familiarity* of feeling unhappy. It's a vicious circle!

Your brain is quite prepared to put up a fight; it's not willing to give up its beloved familiarity easily. The mere possibility of having to face change or an unknown situation delivers enough fuel to fight against leaving the comfort zone. Your subconscious will invest a lot of energy to manipulate any endeavours which might prove hostile. Unknown territory is considered *the* enemy at this point. As a result, you'll find a million and one excuses to not make any changes. The moment a little courage is summoned, the armed brain convinces you that any intended new circumstance can only represent trouble; a huge amount of self-doubt is thrown in for free and all fragile courage disappears into the endless nowhere of your mind. For now, the weird and wonderful brain has won, again.

An unforeseen way to grow
Life often takes de-tours; numerous women can tell a story or two of their own roundabout routes. In an odd way, being stuck in a comfort zone represents such diversion; ultimately it symbolises augmentation though. As soon as certain actions and behaviours

are understood, one can change them. Comfort zones are de-tours only temporarily; they don't automatically imprison one indefinitely. Being a couple of steps ahead of oneself will aid the crucial first move into a comfort zone-free life – it's time to face the mighty brain.

'Uncomfortable' joins forces
There is a surprisingly simple to accomplish exercise aiding the successful tackle of comfort zones. So simple, in fact, one can't but wonder whether there's a catch. What women I have worked with experienced to be the most effective and easily executed way annoys many therapists, as it limits their income opportunities substantially.

To describe its nature reminds one somewhat of the proverb 'Cruel to be kind', as it at its first glance suggests a resemblance. However, kindness will overtake cruelness within moments of its perseverance.

In essence, 'cruel' is easily explained – you *temporarily* need to feel uncomfortable in order to learn to cope with unpleasant situations. The tables need turning – the habit feeling miserable must transform into the habit of feeling *self-confident* when endeavouring challenges. You need not worry; it won't involve dancing around naked. Please assess your *usual* ways; look what you normally do and, even more essential, what you normally don't do. Proven to be the most effective method to experiment with leaving the comfort zone is to do the exact opposite to some of your usual ways. This is for therapeutic and

experimental purposes only and does not represent
any permanent adjustments.

It's simple – if you normally wear your hair down
because you are convinced it's best, wear it up. If you
normally wear it up all the time, wear it down. If you
normally never wear make-up, wear make-up for
experimental purposes. If you normally always do,
leave it off for a week or two. The same goes for clothes
– if you normally never wear a skirt or dress, wear them
now. If you normally never wear trousers, give them a
try. Just one easy and simple change to your 'normal'
way will do wonders for the progress of freeing
yourself – and your brain – from your comfort zone.

What sounds unorthodox and in many fellow
therapists' ears by far too simple *does* work, and these
little day-to-day and simple tasks can prove to be of
immense aid to escape your comfort zone. They will
make you feel slightly uncomfortable, but this emotion
is amply intended. Such action will politely force your
brain to handle new and *uncomfortable* scenarios. This
force is a hassle it could do without, it tries to avoid it
at first, but eventually, it'll learn to adapt. Making sure
you cannot escape your own experiment is a critical
part; if you normally never wear make-up to work,
don't let your brain manipulate you by taking make-
up remover wipes along. Facing such uncomfortable
experience is vital to transform your brain's association
of 'comfortable' with 'avoidance'.

After a while, when escape cannot take place, the
discomfort from wearing make-up as a contrary to

your usual way will automatically trigger the known emotion of familiarity in your brain, with one simple but wonderful side effect – your brain is getting used to these new influences. By *gently* forcing yourself to face an uncomfortable situation you'll learn to get comfortable. Even the scariest things can be tackled this way, one at a time, and self-confidence will grow with every little effort made. It's thorny at first to believe that such tiny temporary changes regarding make-up or clothes can make a difference to the perception of oneself and for the brain to overcome itself, but many women I have worked with found this after all to be quite easily within their capabilities. Sounds too easy to work? The best and most effective solutions are often the simplest – try it.

Only outside your comfort zone change can happen

Any *temporary* change you decide to try for therapeutic reasons automatically represents a stimulating and therefore positive influence; it will help the re-adjustment of your brain to switch from uncomfortable to comfortable. In the case of my friend Irene, we confronted her with the Full Monty – she *normally* never wore lots of make-up, *now* she looked like a parrot. She *normally* never wore skirts, *now* she did, especially short ones. She *normally* never joined her female work-colleagues for a chat in the kitchen, *now* she forced herself to do so and even practised a little harmless and friendly gossiping. Her hair she was ruthless with – she cut her long hair off, transformed her looks, and despite not liking the bob-look she went for, she looked gorgeous. All of a sudden, all eyes were on her for the right reasons.

The motive behind the drastic approach towards her hair was pure; she positively wanted to con herself to stick to change. 'Hair will grow', she said, 'but if I don't cut it off, I'll never go through with wearing it differently. I've always worn it down. And since I hate a bob on me, that's the look I'm going for. I'll feel as uncomfortable as hell.'

I was truly impressed.

Bit by bit Irene achieved to feel more and more comfortable with feeling uncomfortable, and after a while she didn't even notice her change from 'normal' anymore. So remember, the more you feel uncomfortable at first, the better your chances being able to deal with bumpy situations will become. Also remember, feeling uncomfortable is just a bad habit. Remind yourself every time the uncomfortable feeling creeps in, and the moment you feel uncomfortable is the moment to react with courage and determination to win the battle against your impressive brain.

Whatever you choose to temporarily change, it's the exercise itself that's important. You can choose anything you like, as long as it is the *opposite* of your normal way – for as long as it takes to break the habit. Be aware that your brain will try to sabotage your plans to break out, it will try to victimise you before you've even started getting into a skirt in the morning if you normally only ever wear trousers. It will come up with one million and one excuses why *not* to wear a skirt today – the weather is bad, the tummy is bloated, the top is the wrong colour – don't let your brain win. As soon as your brain tells you 'don't' you know your comfort zone is kicking in, and you know it's time to 'do' the exact opposite to how you feel.

Because conflict with yourself always seems easier than confrontation with any unknown territory, your brain is quite an opponent and prefers to battle with the lesser of the threats – *you*. Being aware of this simple fact you already have a great advantage – the data of your brain's intensions prepare you for this fight. Once aware of your brain's manipulation, fighting back becomes straightforward. Try it; you'll be amazed what such an unproblematic method can shift.

Irene, now with a bob, but finally free
After years of struggling with a very low self-esteem and therefore practically non-existing self-confidence, my friend freed herself from her limiting comfort zone completely. All her uncomfortable feelings at work have vanished into nothing more than a distant memory. Breaking with old habits like feeling shy, underdog-like or insecure took a bit of time, but was effort well worth invested. The confrontation with her inner self presented the possibility for exploring her own true potential, even if it had meant chopping off her hair. She's back to wearing trousers only, as she really hates skirts, and to not using any make-up; her new hairstyle, however, she has kept, and she truly looks very chic.

New, never experienced energy, directly resulting from rewarding self-confidence and a healthy attitude, saw her stand up against the obstacles placed by life. Her anxieties diminished and neither being single nor her mother's bossy and overbearing approach to forcing marriage and grandchildren into her life were threatening arguments; they were as dead as ever.

So full of energy close to bursting point, Irene now can't help herself and jump out of tiny flying aeroplanes twice a month – an activity, however madcap, she'd always dreamed of pursuing. During one jump on a sunny Sunday afternoon, plummeting towards Earth at 120 miles per hour, she unexpectedly, and rather literally out of the blue, met Mr. Perfect. He turned out to be her soul mate, and very much to the relief of her mother, they will get married soon. I, on the other, had for self-preservation reasons hoped for a less spectacular celebration of their union, perhaps skipping getting married altogether, as the two have decided to get married plunging from the heavens. Foolishly, I have agreed to function as a witness while being strapped to a tandem jump parachute instructor. Whoever thinks life's dull should take up psychology.

A swift summary
This is only one example of many women I have met who had in common the urge to break free from these strange steel bars; bars they instinctively knew held them back, but which also provided this unexplainable outlandish feeling of support and comfort – comfort zone. Due to bad experiences, scores of women lock themselves away, turn into hermits and avoid anything that might represent an uncomfortable situation. Hiding might seem a good idea at first, but if not careful, the bad habit of feeling dreadful kicks in.

Life will always hold some uncomfortable situations in stock for us; how to handle them is very much down to the individual and the willingness to accept that life is not always pink in colour. A healthy optimism, a good sense of humour and the curiosity to explore successes will lend a helping hand to any woman yearning to make a difference to the inner self.

Many have confirmed it, once you taste the future, it really tastes delicious.

'In my teens I feared, in my twenties
I explored, in my thirties
I misunderstood; now in my forties,
I own the world.'

Carol

Ageing – trauma or deliverance?

The magic and angst of ageing is to be found
everywhere. The manufacturers of anti-ageing
products would miss it greatly, if it ever was to
disappear from women's top ten list of everlasting
worries and irritations. I lost count of how many
women I have met who filled me in on their inner
worries about ageing and how this eventually overtook
their outer beauty, astoundingly reflecting the inner
tumult in facial expressions, overall body posture and
attitude. The fear of ageing can reach proportions most
women didn't know they were capable of arriving at.

This burden is not carried alone – every person on this
planet will inevitably age, and of course this is no
news. Using this ageing fact to gain greater
acceptance, however, doesn't seem feasible at first to
most. Not just the first signs of ageing – grey and
thinning hair, age spots, and wrinkles to name but a
few – make women feel like they're the first to suffer
it; women usually think they're the *only* one facing the

rot. Staying 'young looking' turns into a sporting discipline where the silver let alone bronze medal is not considered acceptable.

The amount of money spent on fighting off the years seems limitless. What is undoubtedly good for the economy is only for a short period of time good for the female ego. It's vital to understand that ageing takes place even with countless beauty products filling domestic bathroom shelves, but of course, this is again no news. The use of approved beauty products like anti-ageing crèmes is certainly much advised, yet crèmes will eventually only smooth the outer self and only for so long. As far as the price tags of beauty products are concerned, the rule of thumb should be spending the respective age in currency, for instance, a forty-five year old lady needn't spend any money in excess of her age - £45. For many, this is already a very expensive luxury – one more reason to re-think the whole ageing scare and to age freely without breaking any budget. I'm not suggesting to not taking care of oneself, far from it. The message, however, is crème-smear free – accept what eventually even crèmes can't prevent from happening.

Ageing can *and should* be seen as a two-sided sword – on the one hand it is a biological reality, unavoidable and probably necessary; on the other hand ageing represents the magnificent opportunity to grow and glow, to become sharper in the true sense of the meaning and should be seen as a mental maturing onto never expected higher grounds when still in the twenties or thirties, unimaginable to a certain extent even way into a woman's forties.

This short chapter takes great pride in reminding women that life, once immune towards absurd external influences, is truly worth living, with 'maturing' easily equalling 'liberation'. Deliverance is on its way and an always longed for freedom will automatically transpire from inner places formally dreaded to brand one as 'old'. In unison with the ever-more crucial inner independence this wisdom delivers untouchability, and this chapter is dedicated to the wonderful discovery of life's path becoming more beautiful with age. Just like maturing wine, maturing women are as enjoyable, if not more – especially once the advanced mind practises the most efficient of all tools – *self-acceptance;* there's honestly nothing quite like it.

The teens – scary, but unavoidable

Girls in their teens are the most misguided people of the planet, shortly after misguided boys, of course. The whole experience of being a teenager, hitting puberty and other nuisances has hopefully by now well bypassed the reader; a time for many not worth remembering, it won't find any further space in this chapter. The whole idea of 'Childhood' and at times the resulting bad experiences, not necessarily having to mean disaster for future adulthood years to come, is covered in the respective chapter in this little book of freedom occupying its worthy spot. For now, our journey takes us to see ageing in a different light.

The twenties – time to explore

Maturing happens in steps, a few at a time. When in their twenties, women tend to believe the world revolts around them; in constant competition with other young women the own place and space in this world is not obvious just yet, although most young women seem to behave as if they knew, of course, everything there's to know about life, men, politics, the environment, world peace and the meaning of it all. Invincibility is greatly assumed to be surrounding young women, yet stubborn insecurities rule at the same time. The desire to hide imperfections rules even more. The journey of life, now legally backed up to include various types of young men, usually consist of the first relationships, the first break-ups, towards the end of the twenties perhaps even the first house purchase and in many cases the first children. If the world of academics was chosen, the early twenties are the years to establish a certain professional path.

Having varying preferences or even just the idea of changing the own opinions or perhaps feeling different one day most young women don't feel the need to waste any brain power on. For most of them the time is now and life is being lived this way. Exploring the inner and outer limits is the key to all meanings and functions as healthy frictions in the lines of 'me against the world'. Luckily, young women will find out all by themselves just how much flux is happing all around at all times; they certainly don't need for more mature women to lead the way.

The thirties – time to misunderstand
The next milestone to be found in their thirties, women the world over realise that life itself is not always what many assumed it would turn out to be when still in the twenties. The first major disappointments are being

registered; men change, jobs change, friends change. The wardrobe changes with the seasons and the first signs of ageing appear miraculously; that life will eventually have a 'best before date' becomes a not so easily to be shifted fact. Various attempts to make good and to compensate for what went wrong regarding men, relationships and other subjects are experimented with, at this stage usually resulting in countless misunderstandings; despite all good intentions, confusion seems to be even more intense that a decade ago.

When already settled in some sort of family arrangement including a man and children, an annoying mother, mother-in-law or both, gardening work and a former boss demanding the return to work after a short maternity leave, the thirties are usually the first important decade delivering realisation that all sorts of obstacles appear on a daily basis. Life might not turn out to be as easily conquerable as it so often had seemed when in the late teens or early twenties. Well in their thirties, it's daunting on many women that life is very short indeed; unhealthy compromises are being identified more than ever before and the urge to find a way out is pretty much on the unhappy mind for lengthy moments of time.

The forties and beyond – immunity and giggles
The forties are the mile stone most women I have worked with find to be the most important. Many are scared about the yet unknown new decade to come, as many women intuitively feel the importance of this time of halfway in one's life. Life has never felt to

move at such quick pace before; Christmas and birthdays seem to take place once a month instead of once a year, the seasons fly by, the kids grow, wisdom does, too. It scares many to experience the fact that midlife, including its crisis's, does, in fact, exist.

Luckily, there are also some women who already see turning forty to be the gratefully appreciated border between insanity and freedom, with freedom starting pretty much at midnight on the 40th birthday. Some say the 40th is the beginning of insanity as well as freedom, now being both, affordable as well as explainable. I leave it to the individual reader to decide which one works best, but I especially love the idea of turning forty being a liberating lunacy. There's hardly anything more therapeutic than celebrating freedom, particularly a few minutes before the big four zero arrives.

Being self-confident and seeing the actions of younger years with careful, older eyes luckily makes wrongdoings, false assumptions and misguided views shrink down to rather insignificant mistakes of the past – they're all part of growing up. This very attitude is the way forward, and will make the difference between one's tomorrow being blunt and limited or indeed interesting, exciting and filled with self-acceptance.

Contrary to many initial assumptions, ageing is very much the best thing that can happen to anybody, but especially to women. All those wonderful personalities I have worked with over the years would now confirm that hitting forty was the most exhilarating experience – it meant *real* life has only just begun.

The right sense of humour has proven to be of gigantic aid – being able to laugh about the way the own perception of life changes is the fundamental first step triggering self-acceptance to evolve. Preferences, those assumed to ever be so important views and plans, outlooks and influences change; what one liked or even loved in the twenties and thirties often crumbles down to not much more than a silly scrutiny of a girl maturing over the years. Women's changing sense for clothes is one perfect example and testament.

I wish I was dead

I lost count of the number of women who have said these few words to me when being asked what brought them to enquire my services in the first place, when 'ageing' was on their mind. To allow the thought of maturing being the utmost liberation requires a confident courage and the never-ending practising of self-acceptance, once more and more than ever. The true inner freedom coming from ageing has to be experienced to be believed – a naked fact many of my younger clients at first wash away as being the gibberish of an old bird like me. The secret is so much more fascinating – not to care about anything surrounding the subject of ageing, feeling the immunity, feeling the inner independence to simply not care anymore about grey hair or wrinkles – young ladies, you're lucky, it will come to you, too.

The tourist in life

When explaining 'life' in its stages as plainly as possible, the following example many women have found to be very helpful in aiding the independent and dependable development of one's inner strength, also delivering a great and humorous solidarity; after all, bodily decomposition certainly having its funny moments can be compensated for with the, once untouchable, unbeatable skill of making fun of oneself.

Hopefully enabling the average woman to see it from her own point of view one day, the maturing process can pretty much be seen like visiting a big and juicy city. New York is the perfect example; countless women of all ages have visited this invigorating place. Those who fell in love with it and who have visited it regularly over their lifetime can co-incidentally discover how their interest in New York over the decades of visiting the Big Apple changes. The fascination remains, but the *perception* transforms in more than one way, ultimately, however, resulting in a relaxed freedom and comforting peace of mind of how to explore the City – therefore being synonymous to exploring life.

New York is full, literally full of interesting sights and museums, theatres, nightlife, markets with shopping opportunities, art galleries, cinemas, bookstores, jewellery shops and endless more things to be done and experienced. It's not an overstatement to say that one could stay in New York for a whole long year, explore something different every single day and not doing anything twice while there. That's how vast New York is – just like life.

Indeed, life *is* like New York, full of interesting things. Sights, museums and so on all metaphorically stand for one adventure in life, like relationships, men in general, family planning, experimenting with different professional approaches and countless endeavours more. New York has also as many one-way street systems, tunnels, subways and construction sites, forcing many to negotiate detours, as life itself has to offer.

When visiting New York, for instance for the first time in the twenties, the interested traveller feels obliged and almost obsessed to visit everything, or at least as much as humanly possible. Early morning starts to make sure the planned activities are standing a chance of being ticked off the to-do list are anticipated with excitement and wonderful expectations of what the day might bring, followed by evening entertainment and dancing through the night, *especially* when in the twenties.

Then, when returning in one's thirties, the lust to see and experience New York is still strong; the visit is looked forward to immensely, yet once one arrives, the urge to cram everything in all of a sudden loosens up compared to the previous visit. Different sights and activities now demand attention and take over the priority list of things to be done, visited, explored and purchased, and all at a slower pace. The best part about it, however, is the strange comfort to be at ease with it – after all, one has successfully completed a tour of most of the places of interests before. The relaxation kicking in and the realisation to not be obsessed with the sights anymore causes one to see different things with different eyes – gratefulness to be less obsessive soothes the mind historically known as 'wild'. A weird, certain relief is being felt, and enjoyed. New York is seen in a different, yet still very sexy light.

The miracle of maturing metamorphosis is complete when being in the forties and visiting one of the most fascinating places in the world once again. After having been here in the twenties, after having seen most of what there is to see and after re-visiting a decade later, this visit, however, carries the utmost of all travel satisfaction – to be able to simply breathe in and take in the atmosphere of New York. The opinion having to pack in as much as possible has changed completely; not only has most stuff on offer been done already, the ability to now choose wisely where to go back to, *if at all,* brings liberation of previously unknown proportions. A stress-free trip like this provides not just a solace of great importance to travelling; visiting New York is the perfect metaphor of how life works during the female's minds' journey from 'young, innocent and misguided' to 'mature, wonderful and free'.

The point of no return
It is sad how many women get stressed out over ageing – not just physically, that eventually seems to be the least of one's worries. It's the inner fear or inner moulder that most often paralyses women to see the funny, and lots more important, the uplifting and liberating side of maturing. When asked if they would love to turn back time from their forties to their twenties, women intuitively, so it seems, rush

to answer this trick-question with a quick and enthusiastic 'yes, please!'. However, when being introduced to looking at maturing as a liberating gift, and looking at the New-York-equals-life-example, many have changed their perception within moments. Too tempting is the thought that the forties and years beyond by far are more interesting than the twenties – *and they are.*

The little reminder in this little book of freedom is usually all it took to convert the women I have worked with from fearing the big four zero to hardly being able to wait. Once this liberation is tested one will never want to time travel back ever again. Too much true fun was to be found in life living it with the fun-factor rather than the fear-factor; true self-acceptance regarding this and other major subjects like weight scares, nicotine scares and more, further discussed in the last chapter of this book, bears such enormous powers, women I have introduced to seeing their life like a trip to New York became unstoppable even to my surprise; I'm not usually surprised easily – but some of my clients have blown even my established views overboard and have revealed personalities I wouldn't think were possible to find within, truly proving that life is indeed a voyage of discovery.

Being able to laugh off any charming quirkiness, the first forgetfulness, the already discussed physical signs of loving corrosion as well as the first time getting out of bed with every bone in the body being painful is the most resourceful and valuable aid to grow old, both gracefully and stylishly. A few bumps here or there might be a verification of senses weakening, yet at the same time being at ease with it is one of the most attractive sides in a woman. Being able to forgive oneself for the mistakes made in an ancient past supports this wonderful metamorphosis. Chuckling and giggling about self-inflicted but hilarious situations and scenarios are female weapons of absolutely unconquerable qualities.

As in all chapters before, the most effective and innovative, idiot-prove and usable advice is the shortest. This chapter, as the others, would love to deliver certain food for thought, motivation to re-think the too often occurring inner panic attacks and most importantly encourage changing the view of ageing the next time an inner scare is allowed to have a voice. A little soul-searching has never done any harm and will give some soon to be discovered and inspiring waves a good vibe in the fine old soul.

The next time you're feeling blue about too many pounds on your hips, too many wrinkles in your face, cellulite on your bottom, an aching back, thinning hair, age spots and all the other side effects and punches to vanity occurring with age – think again. As much as anybody with an appropriate budget can buy useful help to slow ageing down, the *true inner beauty* is not available on any store shelves.

So remember, naturally given youth is a gift with a short shelf life; women like Margaret Rutherford, an amazing lady of substance who had only come to fame in her fifties and who, in absence of advanced skin care, was already pretty wrinkly, have never bothered denying this and still will never be seen as old or horrible, but as immune to any anti-ageing wars, a fact filling many maturing women with jealousy. If we allow an already existing inner growth to develop and expand though, pair it with not giving a damn about what will evidentially sooner or later happen to all of us and sprinkle over a good sense of humour to make fun of oneself we should be armed for life to eventually rot away, if only on the outside.

Your inside, however, is untouchable; *how much you let it fight for or against you is up to you.*

**"Family' reminds me of a flock of sheep.
You stick together
when the wolves are around,
but you do hope all the others
go to the abattoir before you.'**

Nora

Family – escaping from wolf *and* abattoir

Certainly in the top ten of the most popular nuisances
to complain about is the subject of 'family' or next
of kin, ancestors, folks, relatives, relations to name
but a few other nouns to summarise this institution.
Fathers, mothers, brothers, sisters, grandfathers,
grandmothers, uncles, aunts, nephews, nieces, and
cousins are just the first in line to claim the positions of
members of your family. Then, in the next line, we can
put a 'grand' in front of a few positions – grandfather,
grandmother,... The next line after that puts a 'step' in
front of every noun – stepbrother, stepsister,...

Sometimes, one has all three lines at once to deal
with, and before one can say 'my dynasty', the
number of people in the immediate family might near
the one hundred mark, which makes weddings and
christenings ridiculously expensive.

I have met dozens of women who would have loved
to either behead or strangle or do something of a

similar evil outcome to many of their family members, especially to their parents. Women of any age, but particularly when in their late thirties or even early forties were on the brink of madness because of family members trying to interfere with their lives on a level beyond impartial, loving or caring advice.

The most often occurring constellation of trouble I have found to be between mothers and daughters, closely followed by sibling friction and cousin to cousin jealousies and concluding in the overall disaster of countless grandmothers' attempts to dictate the future blood line of the family. Fighting about female dress sense in addition to food preferences drives women in later years to longing to put Granny's head into the food processor twice a month.

Historically, family was and still is seen to be a union and community of people sharing the same blood, or at least some sort of paperwork with their names on it, and is to provide comfort and security, shelter and affection, sanctuary and peace for one another. The idea of 'family' should give a feeling of wellbeing in heart and mind, should make us feel appreciated, loved, supported and cared for. When things regarding 'family' turn out well in a woman's life, it's a brilliant institution to call upon.

What sounds so wonderful is strictly speaking – and very unfortunately – a picture of the past and simply not the naked reality for far too many of us. If you have a superb and supportive family as described, and millions of fortunate women no doubt do, you should consider yourself incredibly blessed and therefore enjoy both, the thought of them being a pleasant part of your life as well as having them around for Sunday lunch, if you wish to do so. Many of your fellow women in today's world are not that lucky, and this chapter is intended to encourage the untoward souls on the verge to committing a crime to experiment with a new approach to address an at times overbearing pressure. To minimise restrictive compromise and to maximise liberating independence is the objective.

'I only want your best, dear'

On top of the complaints list of the relationships between mothers and daughters we'll find the mother's isolated ideas of how to lead a life, her daughter's life, to be precise. A great deal of energy, time and effort is regularly invested into convincing the own flesh and blood about the important necessities and forbidden fruits in life, certainly and solely linked to one's mother's own point of view, and why any other vision can only ever be deemed wrong. Boyfriend or husband, girlfriend or civil partner, the chosen job, the decision to have children or not, the chosen wall paper for the living room or even the favourite hair colour of the month – mothers feel shockingly free to criticise and complain about their daughters, at any rate driving the off-spring into despair – and into preventable compromises. Bi-monthly quarrels become predictable, and when it happens, it seems to happen never-endingly.

Very often the daughter finds herself under constant pressure and feels obliged to meet demands. Although

barely agreeing with any of her mother's views, she
adamantly yields to the enlightening attempts of
the senior, merely to avoid any harmony to be
destroyed any further. After long and loud clashes
and following the humble advice of a once read
proverb, the daughter decides the smarter one gives in.
Ultimately, off-putting compromises begin to embrace
her; with every Sunday Roast another compromise can
be added to the list. Driven by frustration, ever more
clever reasons to avidly avoid any get-togethers creep
in. Emotionally, this is a boomerang getting faster
and faster to hit both parties fully face on, eventually.
With every single argument the daughter's longing
wish being spared from the mother's views grows.
It's now only a matter of time for things to deteriorate
completely.

Mothers want the so-called best for their daughters;
often they want for them what hasn't been achieved in
their own lives, like finding Mr. Perfect or pursuing a
better job. The list of reasons to disagree over is very
long, whether it's mothers and daughters or any other
combination of family members feeling the need to
have an opinion where perhaps they shouldn't.

Friction, confusion and lots of people
The 'mothers and daughters' scenario is only one
simple example, but functions as best illustration.
A whole book of family disasters alone could easily be
filled, as it's one of the most often named annoyances
in today's women's lives and effortlessly made it to
the top ten list. The bottom line is that disagreeing
family members once too often arguing generate

emotions and urges to jump at each other's throats. Many women, particularly younger ladies, not being blood-related but still being required to acknowledge a 'stepmother' or a 'stepfather' certainly don't face trouble-free happy family situations.

Let's face it – the regular picture of 'nowadays families' doesn't automatically bear a resemblance to the charming picture of the past. Unconditional love is much desired, yet seldom granted. These days, families are too often split; many people living under one roof with more than just one surname is standard. Postal workers find this as confusing as registry staff in the local surgeries does. A woman having three children, each with a different family name, might seem unorthodox to some, but it happens repeatedly. Step-parents and stepchildren mixing but not necessarily matching, great-grandmothers looking after their granddaughter's stepchildren's ex-partners newborn and even more uncanny, or modern, an uncle accompanying his nephew's new girlfriend's ex-stepson from a just broken down relationship to the dentist to fix some braces – it's confusing, to say the least, and who wants to blame who for being emotionally puzzled, let alone forgetful about surnames?

The face of a modern family might look entertaining at first, but it's, to be more accurate, more than bizarre – for the lack of a better word, it's even frenetic, in an endearing and chaotic way. The very sense of security and shelter, support and warmth has long gone for so many people, and the lack of it can only be considered a part of the new face of today's family life.

Care or chaos?
However, a focal point of this very strange arrangement called 'Family in the 21st Century' is still somewhat the wellbeing of the people we share a name with, or not. Whether we share the housing arrangements and letter boxes or the gardens for summer time barbecues, we try our best to welcome all those faces we can't always recognise instantaneously into our midst. If we are lucky, we might be assured by a more informed aunt that all those faces are somewhat now related by some paperwork, including children stemming from relationships long gone and further stepchildren at the same time. Despite these confusions, the welfare of all family members involved remains an intuitive focal point.

The involved contribution to a family member's comfort and happiness is therefore usually well intended. However, this deliberate involvement in another person's life too often looks and feels a lot like snooping around in very private areas, engages giving unasked advice and opinions, implicates bossing one around and leads to arguing endlessly over many things including trivia. This mere participation of others drives countless women into experiencing the previously unknown compulsion to chop off heads and boiling them in salt water. If you feel like numerous of great women I have worked with over the years and find yourself in such state of affairs, here's good news – you are not alone.

'Do we really have to go?'
One-to-one problems, like mothers and daughters, or big family gatherings – I have experienced many

adventures, and there's no lesser word for it, and witnessed quite a few of those jamborees with first, second and third connecting lines as well as not yet identified new lines of so-called family members. My own barmy family as well as witnessing crazy relatives of friends, the madness occurring during these occasions has often left me wondering about the yet rather limited number of murders committed within domestic barbecue or Sunday Roast settings.

Everybody talking at the same time when families get together is no news, especially when the majority of people present are women and girls of all ages, but it usually was the proprietary approach they had to one another I found the most interesting to watch from a safe distance. All calm at first, upon arrival various little groups start harmless chats - mothers compare nappy brands; fathers compare football teams; grandparents compare life prior to and after various wars; young children compare gadgets nobody else could operate; young teenage girls compare boy bands; young teenage boys compare skateboards; girls in their late teens compare themselves and boys of similar age compare the girls as well – so far, so good.

Every time, anywhere amidst large unlucky family gatherings and not long after arrival, the polite approach to one another usually fades and whatever is closest to one's heart will be shared, whether others want to hear about it or not. Quarrels break loose, arguments rule and everyone present longs to be hiding is holes in the ground – or to be leaving. In families with an unfortunate amount of harmony remaining it is common place for many women desiring to run a mile when the email invite makes its round, in due course hoping to avoid confrontations. To *not* get involved – if only they knew how without hurting family members' feelings – occupies countless female brains in the run-up to any assembly.

Odd fact

Seen by many as a highly controversial issue and not commonly accepted, the liberating and uncomplicated truth is you don't have to love your family. You don't even have to *like* them – but you have to act accordingly. *The advice is simple* and many of my peers find this to be too nonconformist to be introduced; I, however, have found it to undoubtedly work finest for countless women – if you don't like your family, either just one person or all of them, accept it. Don't force yourself to change your attitude or belief, just because you're dealing with 'family'. A false sense of guilt and a forced and inherited compassion for blood relatives misguide our emotions, suppressing our real wishes and tightly wrapping us in limiting compromises, with every meeting a little tighter. The often well-meant yet very annoying interfering of 'family' with one's choices and preferences drives innumerable women of any age to breaking point. Too many accept this circumstance, despite being very unhappy about it. The lack of courage and ultimately the lack of self-confidence to face the differences between 'family' and the 'self' prevent too many women from escaping infuriating scenarios. Unhealthy compromises become part of a typical family face, and this face naturally lacks any genuine, caring smiles and loving grins.

'My choice, Mum, remember?'

The list of irritations is long, but one apt example of mother – daughter disagreement is the never-ending line of reasoning of having or not having children. I could introduce dozens of women who feel that motherhood is just not for them. Femininity is not exclusively signified by breeding; this is a ruthless myth from the past. Some women simply don't want the commitment of children, prefer a lifestyle not ideal for any offspring and decide to not have kids at all. Some women toy with the idea of having children, yet the man ultimately intended to share this adventure with hasn't been found in a rational biological timeline. Other women get irritable just looking into the direction of a pram and want to run a mile for no reason other than simply not finding the concept of pushing something as big as a watermelon through something as small as a lemon appealing. However, being sensible and sound about this subject does not often receive the potential grandmothers' sanction.

The women concerned usually experience some insult to their intelligence and decision making abilities, whether it's baby-related or connected to any other subject. Often they have to live through showers of well-meant advice on various issues, eventually finding themselves excusing, justifying and explaining their motives for living an heir-free or any other independent life; a position all women lacking deeply desired self-confidence and thick skin share. Bad compromises spread once more and anguish deepens.

Truly self-governing decisions

The overall idea is to develop a nice immunity and
untouchability towards any outside and often obscure
pressures – 'family' is one of them. Whether they
like it or not, 'family' have, strictly speaking, no
right whatsoever to agree or disagree, approve or
disapprove with anything one does with their adult
life – no right at all.

The individual choice of lifestyle, an independent
choice of friends and partners, any particular choice of
how to spend hard-earned money *and any other choices
one could possibly relate to* – whatever creates and
supports one's happiness should be followed with
persevering assertiveness, as no need for anybody to
approve of anything is given. The controversial advice
is again a simple one – risk to upset people, even if it
means distressing family members. This demonstration
of independence sooner or later will fill even the most
stubborn family with pride to have bred such self-
reliant woman.

Blackmail – beware

Emotional blackmail is a common form of expressing
the disappointment with one's decisions and deeds,
most often occurs when parents and children disagree
and usually transpires once all other efforts to
influence an intended direction fail. Any parent
hoping to achieve certain authority by blackmailing
their children through a variety of enormous
pressures expresses a very mean abuse of emotion
and power. The extents range from putting on Oscar-
worthy movie performances playing old, frail and

dying mothers and fathers to tempting the own flesh and blood with ridiculous amounts of money and anything of similar enormity in between to ensure a continued part-take in one's life – emotional fangs around many women's necks, truly suffocating them. To address this, the advice is simple once more – anybody trying to emotionally blackmail another person should be informed frankly that such inadequate action is not going unnoticed and is highly unappreciated. Being polite, but straight is essential. However, bear in mind that nobody, not even parents have the right to play one for a fool. The sooner this is understood, the quicker independence will grow.

Independence, not compromise

It is widely gazed at as perhaps an outlandishly novel view, but the naked truth remains unchallenged – let's remember, family members, despite the old-fashioned 'blood is thicker than water' gibberish, don't have to love or even like anybody in their own lineage; being somewhat related either by nature or paperwork doesn't justify any self-sacrifice or disengagement from own beliefs and practices. It's another of those erstwhile myths passed from one generation to the next, running through one's life like an alarming red ribbon; the older generations swayed the younger ones that loving your own kin was mandatory and equalled respect. Saying 'yes, father' does not automatically show a true respect; back in the old days, it purely stood for 'fear of father'; an occurrence many elderly women can confirm. Once essential to ensure family survival, those times have long gone. Growing the self-confidence to stand up for oneself is lots healthier than ever-embracing compromises. To declare with confidence if one finds certain family members worth chopping into pieces is the first important step.

Too many times in too many women's lives these noxious compromises dictate the scenes, merely in absence of courage to say 'stop' or 'no'. Excuses are made in one's head to justify the lack of revolt when, once more and once again, the own lifestyle is firmly criticised. The most common hesitation is linked to feelings of guilt and over-sensitive compassion, in the end resulting in sentimental obligation and an overwhelming fear to hurt the person, usually a parent, concerned. For many a surprise, but 'love and respect' for mother and father is purely an educated dogma, and sadly has driven plenty of women with unfortunate family relations, especially a challenged parent–child relationship, into suicide. In the wild world of Mother Nature, the ties between parents and offspring usually disappear, turning mothers and daughters into strangers to one another. Although it doesn't have to stretch to such extent, to live completely independently if so desired is perfectly acceptable, in spite of common morals.

It being regarded as an affront to disobey or disagree with parents provides these closest of all relatives with power over their children, *even after reaching adulthood* – hence parents the world over can so very successfully abuse emotions for blackmail purposes. Despair and further rigid developments in the already crooked relationship are widespread. The hesitation of

a daughter telling her mother off for once and for
all too often is merely due to the overwhelming angst
to stand up against the system of belief. It's strongly
recommended to *not* compose further excuses or
delays, no matter how bizarre this advice might
seem; to communicate openly if boiling point has
been reached and expressing with pride that
absolutely none of your life choices resemble any
wrongdoing will assist distressed minds to accept
your independence. Also, the effortless yet true-life
pièce de résistance accepting 'live and let live' as a
karma has proven to be a great backing.

No family is perfect
In an ideal world, women everywhere would prefer to
have family contact in any shape or form because they
want to have this contact, not because they *have* to
have it. The feeling of obligation has long ago taken
over the emotion of true delight, degrading the visits
of parents or grandparents into a mere bullet point on
a bi-monthly agenda. Some say these visits equal a lie,
as they resemble a close link to an action not executed
voluntarily.

The acceptance to not have the best of all families is
of crucial importance and is the most effective and
aiding tool; it supports finding an individual way out
of arms that limit rather than embrace affectionately.
Unfairly, this advice is often seen as cruel by some
overly soft, compromisingly weak and dishonest
people, especially when ageing parents of older
generations are concerned; claiming to love their
children dearly, they often fail to recognise when it's

time to let go. Perhaps it would help to inform parents that 'letting go' does not equal a 'loss'.

Over the years I have conducted many surveys and studies about the whole family subject; it came into light and was no surprise to me that eight out of ten women compromise greatly and unprofitably when it comes to 'family'. Not saying what they normally would, not wearing what they normally would, not even eating or drinking what they normally would are only very few and rather harmless examples of suppression happening in many wonderful women's family lives.

Liberation is the key – once more
There are countless women who have a wonderful relationship with their family, especially with their parents. Such bad things as blackmail or any other unreasonable pressure would never cross either of the happy parties' minds to use against each other. Those women who are fortunate enough to have been born and raised in such comforting circumstances are very lucky indeed and countless women gaze at such harmony with jealousy.

This chapter, as mentioned at the beginning, is devoted to the many wonderful women who have not had such luck. Not many options are available to them as far as 'change' or 'relief' of any family meddling is concerned. The only attainable way is controversial, perhaps, but indisputably the only frank solution to this strangling problem, which, if unaddressed, will worsen – you have to break free.

How? Practise self-confidence; identify, fight off and become immune to emotional blackmail; demonstrate sovereignty; summon every possible inch of courage; forget old and ill dogmatic practices; send out an emotional rescue team consisting of independent thoughts and actions; stop worrying about what others might think and *change what people see* – wake up to what and who *you* are and reject people's visions of what *they* want to look at.

Only if we make changes change can happen. All these attributes were already standing by within many women I have worked with; unleashing them was all it took to achieve change. Also, every single one celebrated in great relief once this crucial and one of the most desired liberations had been achieved.

The saying goes you can't choose your family – but you *can* choose the extent of their involvement. If you decide less is more, it's legitimate. Trying to convince others about what's right or wrong is a game at times claiming its toll. Every so often, a high price for achievements has to be paid.

Luckily, it's worth it.

'Women are not from
Venus and men are not from Mars.
It's worse than that.
While Venus and Mars are at least
in the same galaxy, women and men are not.'

Katherine

Relationships and Men –
necessity or just 'funny things'?

The number of books written on relationship issues
is so vast that I gave up researching on how many
there are available on the worlds book markets.
The individual subjects covered span from how
relationships work or not work, how to revive being
in love, how to improve living together in general,
how to cope once children have been born, how to
identify differences between female and male
communication systems and probably about one
million other specialised sub-issues. The subject of
'relationships' is, for the lack of a better word, cosmic.

This chapter will not follow into the footsteps of any
of the already established theories and practices.
To simply repeat any of the facts is not the intension of
this division; neither is it necessary nor sensible.
It rather aims to shine as an overall reflection of
one big challenge and the possible consequences
this challenge might bring along with it, as many

magnificent female personalities have experienced. Their relationship hick-ups revolving and revolting around various men all incorporated, amongst a few minor dilemmas, basically just *one big catch.*

My approach is often called 'new', yet I find it not truly 'new' as such; I have, however, found it to be too often much forgotten. As so many times before, this chapter is intended as simple reminder and encouragement fuelling the idea to re-assess or re-evaluate the own inner self and needs; it has in mind to deliver an outlook differentiating the supposedly 'wrongs' and 'rights' in a relationship and whether any overlapping points of interest are indeed lived wrongly or rightly by the two individuals a relationship consists of. After identifying the *one* limiting cage, a cage, however, with many faces, countless women, I'm pleased to say, have come to the re-assuring conclusion that life without a relationship is also, indeed, very easily possible and often repre-sents a previously not considered alternative.

This brief advance also wants to outline that women and men are perhaps strangers to one another by nature; with all the differences the two sexes have to overcome it's easy to see why the world so often refers to them as incompatible. Nevertheless, there's hope and lots more than just any 'wrongs' or any 'rights' to investigate. The strange truth is, in fact, there is *no* 'wrong' or 'right'.

It being a good start, I have met numerous women who already have learnt with the years and with relationships coming and going that there's actually indeed neither a 'wrong' or a 'right', but in essence rather a 'you fit' and a 'you don't fit.' The whole 'Venus' – 'Mars' comparison might sketch a few of these differences, however, most women I have worked with confirmed they don't find this expression to be overflowing with accuracy, hence the statement that women and men are, strictly speaking, not just from different planets, but from different galaxies. One can't but wonder why nature has designed hypothetically two of a kind to be so diverse; living together in alleged harmony dreadfully often and seemingly inevitably develops into a disastrous life-circumstance full of limits and often unavoidable agitation.

Can't live with them, can't live without them?
Relationships and red shoes have a few things in common – at some point in a woman's life they become a necessity, are even yearned for, will always remain perfectly difficult to choose and sooner or later will prove to be useless, inadequate and straightforwardly unsuitable. Being desperate for something makes one adopt an unhealthy compromise at times, too often too many times, and sees women agree to buy weird shoes or enter weird relationships.

Whenever women came to see me and found themselves in an overall good life, it was usually the issue of 'relationships' that proved to have the most room for improvement. Good ones, bad ones and anything going in the middle caused too many women to despair over the subject; the need for a little guidance became obvious very quickly. As in chapters before the best advice is sweet and brief, delivers food for thought and is usable. The overall idea of identifying 'you fit' versus 'you don't fit' in a relationship is the one and only approach that incorporates both, fairness and reason and is the punch line I'd like to concentrate on.

Most relationships seem to be a normal part in a woman's life; one grows up and older, one has the first kisses, partnerships, split-up's and so on. Relationships are greatly considered a normal element in the average woman's existence. Everybody at the same time knows and confirms that relationships are not an easy union, need constant work and apart from very few relationships which seem to hold things together in a weirdly effective way usually end up in a split, for many lots more than just once or twice. What historically was supposed to represent the blending and combination of two people for either a very long time or in some cases even for life no longer seems to carry this specific idyllic nature. Break-ups are as normal as consuming Fish & Chips; both are also not always good for us but often seem to be a welcome necessity.

'You're wrong, darling.' – 'So are you, honey.'
The main reason why relationships seem to fail, annoy, stress, bring to tears, drive one crazy or emotionally kill women is the overwhelming evidence of *total incompatibility* of the female and the male involved in the so-called relationship. The different tastes in TV

programmes, the different understanding of who's in charge of the remote control, which radio stations to tune into, which way to drive to the shopping centre, what to watch in the cinema or going to the cinema at all, which take-away to order, shall we have red wine or beer, sex with lights on or off, the personal driving style, eating slowly or quickly, being close to a panic attack just thinking about travelling by plane together, wanting a family or a more independent lifestyle, money issues, postcodes, nights out or in, smoking or not smoking, political directions, ambitions and dreams, plans and assertiveness, reading before sleeping, separate bedrooms in order to at least get some sleep (snoring!) and seemingly countless other ordinary day-to-day irritations involving the natural overlap of a woman and a man and their different ideas about how to do what, when and why are the strongest indication of whether or not the two of you are likely to have a long-term future or, in fact, no future at all.

The one important factor, the *only* important factor to look out for is the acceptance that there are as a matter of fact no wrongs and no rights – the *only* aspect that matters is to allow the information about the 'you fit' and the 'you don't fit' to find a way into the relationship *and* of course to act accordingly. If two people fit it'll work; if they don't fit it won't work. Trying to shape or educate, re-arrange or influence *the other person* (the partner) or force changes *for* the other person (in the own self) is not only the completely dishonest approach, but will ultimately only suppress the partner or oneself, resulting only in more and

more complicated worries and troubles. Women
or men find themselves so often confronted with
situations causing them to become 'unnatural' in
their own rights, it becomes almost a miraculous
act to recognise the own personality amongst this
emotional mayhem.

Nobody should have to *change* or *behave differently* to
normal, whatever the individual considers to be
'normal', just so they fit or suit another person. The
moment one finds they have to more and more change
or behave differently to their usual ways the end may
as well be believed to be nigh as the number of days,
weeks, months or years for the life expectancy of
the relationship are counted indeed. Often not
recognisable to the naked eye, the countdown towards
the end of the relationship has often already started
long before it's assumed to head the wrong direction.

Many couples I have worked with bend backwards –
in other words agree to live with countless *unhealthy*
compromises – as aberrant individuals, biting their
nails or bits and pieces of hair if long enough, certainly
biting their tongues to avoid confrontation, while
strictly speaking their inside is close to bursting with
the true thoughts, emotions and desires to break the
mould of being limited by the incompatibility of the
partner. Female self-discipline receives a lot of
practice to not lose one's temper.

Incompatible equals incurable?
Whatever the individual preferences are, red wine or
beer; the TV being switched on all day or only ever

reading books; sleeping in or jogging at five o'clock in the morning and a million and one other examples, there's nothing wrong with any of these personal choices, choices every person has the right to choose freely from. However, for a relationship, the more incompatibilities develop over time the more the 'not fitting' will outline that mismatches can stand in the way in the long run.

To identify the *lack* of overlapping personalities, to develop the guts to bring vital points to the attention of the partner and to make a decision accordingly is not easy, yet it is possible. As many times before, self-confidence is all it comes down to when having to handle such tricky situations. Life being too short for major irritations was often illumination enough for many women I have worked with to gather all courage from within and change what drives one mad – a liberation highly recommended, for the sake of everybody. It might sound drastic, but continuing to search for the perfect match is, in fact, the only true cure to relationship troubles.

The bonus thing
Over the years, I have advised countless women to change the plain view and natural value of the relationship they're in from seeing it as a necessity, like trying to catch eight hours of beauty sleep a night, to seeing it as a mere bonus if one's lucky enough to have found the compatible partner.

Learning to live completely without a relationship, at least in one's mind, for any length of time and

hopefully when in between relationships, bears
the quality and benefit of being less obsessed with
finding the 'right' man and frees up more brain power
allocated to tracking down a partner incorporating
both, the soul mate who's on the same wave length
and well as the partner one feels they can be 'at home'
with; being able to be 'yourself' in a partnership
without the need to please the partner unnaturally
is the one and only clue one needs to look out for
to detect any relationship's durability. To *not*
compromise *unhealthily* is the main quality a
relationship has to deliver.

The differences between the types of compromises
were briefly mentioned in the foreword of this little
book of freedom, and of course life is never actually
without any compromises. The *variation* though is to
be found in the tiny detail about any give and take
being of a healthy (beneficial) or unhealthy (limiting)
nature for both parties involved. A healthy compromise is good; an unhealthy one is bad. Different
personas in different women will always have more
than just one or two ideas about a 'good' and a 'bad'
middle ground. Then again, all have in common the
comprehension that any limits causing the inner self to
go beyond recognisable can't but be unhealthy.

Women and men want different things from a
relationship; of course this is no news. Women's
desire to find the right man made many go out
of their ways to accommodate a partner who,
strictly speaking, was unsuitable from the beginning –
a bit like buying red shoes; they don't quite match

the lipstick but were considered an absolute must.
Sooner or later the mismatching colours are *all*
one pays attention to – the time to change the
man, lipstick or the pair of red shoes has come,
once again.

Unless a woman changes her attitude towards
relationships to such drastic length as Rachel has
in the chapter 'Being single – bad luck or great
privilege?' women will continue to work their
way through the telephone directory in search of
the next man. Changing the nature of the search from
looking for the 'usual' man to the 'fitting' man will
make the quest at times perhaps a bit more ruthless,
however in the long run it will relief any lady's
shoulders of a huge amount of pressure. In addition,
to focus on life possibly spent alone yet willing to
engage in a relationship if the *fitting* partner comes
along will take further weight off any woman's mind
– more time to test out 'one fits' can now be assigned
and the subconscious becomes a great ally. After
all, only the own inside really knows what one is
truly after.

I'm unhappy – what next?
If you're one of the dozens of women I have worked
with over the years who is not quite sure where to
take the relationship from its current position to any
possible, preferably better and more fulfilling future –
or to a quick end, it might be time to assess your
involvement and the level of unhealthy compromising
you might already be stuck with. There're a few simple
tricks available to help one find out.

Money

The quickest and most revealing way to find out more is to ask yourself the simple question whether or not you'd leave him if you had all the money in the world. If you're answer is likely to be 'yes, I'd leave if I had that kind of money' you might say aloud what you've always suspected – the two of you simply don't overlap efficiently. Remember, you're neither wrong nor right for each other, *you merely don't fit.* Any relationship being held on to due to the subject of 'money' shows a clear indication for it to end sooner or later. What might seem complicated can work with a bit of effort. Many women have found it uplifting to change the spending schemes within their relationships, enabling a financial independence to grow as soon as somehow feasible.

As much as money is often the reason why some otherwise superficially suitable relationships are wonky, many women, once encouraged to read between the own endlessly repeated lines, find their lives being limited by a few more unhealthy compromises than just the disagreement over or lack of financial means. Often an indicator, too often it is the reason why women put up with what they hate most – the incompatibility stemming from the Frog they're living with, fuelled by hope he might one day turn into a Prince. I have met women who have held back their true inner selves regarding almost anything and everything their men either said, suggested or did – completely and utterly undermining their own preferences, principles and individuality.

When undetected or unsolved women trapped in this kind of relationship will sooner or later try to find solace someplace else. Most find it in other men, many enter a relationship with bottles of wine or other alcoholic friends and still others decide to hide in comfort zones. To get out is the healthiest of all available options, even if it at first seems impossible to achieve, especially when a woman has children to take into account. But it is possible, even now, to become independent. To only dream about a new life is not good enough; to actively work on it is the best idea. Life simply cannot be sacrificed for anything one generally detests and within the own soul has been declared second best.

If a woman has enough independent financial means and stays on despite the relationship being filled to the rim with limiting emotional cages it's strongly suggested to take a closer look into the motives for hanging around. The chapter dedicated to the comfort zones within women might provide a further and often deeply desired insight. Often unknown, but one's misery can become a nasty habit; wonky relationships are frequently linked to situations transforming a little day-to-day trouble into developing an outright comfort zone; once stuck in one of those vicious zones leaving will become more and more difficult.

Misery diary
Unexpected but often to be valued as a truly good friend, some women have found keeping a 'misery diary' to be a good tool aiding the assessment of the

inner attitude towards the man of the moment and the relationship one is in. Writing down all negative emotions linked to day-to-day life and even to life away from any routine, for instance when on holiday, might eventually help identifying the true nature of one's inner commitment. The thicker the diary becomes the more one should re-think the whole matter of 'relationship' with a particular man. Reading about one's individual misery from an outside delivers an insight often overlooked when fighting with ordinary nuisances on a daily basis. Trying this very easily accomplished, affordable mini-therapy has countless times supported women in realising just how much the male might be unsuitably fitting.

The thought of 'another woman' – a weird aid

A few of my colleagues call me mad for suggesting this idea as an aid to investigate one's relationship further. All I do, however, is use already existing emotions for analytical purposes. Meant to be exclusive to one another, all women find the thought of the own man being unfaithful an absolute horror, and of course that's no news. However, this horror-emotion is a strange ally in detecting one's commitment to the partner. In short, if one can imagine the own man in the arms of another woman or even in another bed and doesn't freak out but feels strangely light, perhaps almost relieved, it can be taken as a clear sign that the relationship will come to an end sooner or later. Rather than seeing this as an infuriating suggestion, it has proven countless times to be a very welcomed but underestimated measuring tool detecting the red, orange and green flickering beams of the relationship traffic light. The more 'red' one sees – the more stuck one is.

If he leaves

According to my own statistics the average man only leaves when there's an incentive of quite significant importance waiting at the other end for him; that incentive is usually another woman – not exclusively, but most often. For a man to leave involves lots more effort than for women; all the women I have met who have been left by a man were almost shocked, to avoid the word 'amused', to see just how much fuss seems to be linked to his permanent departure.

Some men, so I and many others have found, worry about leaving on a completely different level than women, which comes as no surprise, as men's wiring is totally different to women's; of course their exits are planned and executed in other ways. I suppose only men can leave a certain time of their lives behind the way they do...

Whatever strange fuss one's man might make, being left means having to re-arrange one's whole life. Everything, absolutely everything one can possibly think of will change, which is of course neither any news nor unheard of. What now matters, however, is a focussed new concentration on an also new and formerly not intended level, a level usually firmly criticised by many.

Despite all the sorrow, make it simple, keep it simple, because it *can* be simple – *be selfish*. Put yourself first, be focussed on yourself, soul search what really matters to you, re-evaluate your interests, your plans, even your immediate surroundings – be self-seeking. Once the dust settles it's very possible you change your views on relationships; many of the women I have worked with became to a certain extent new people with many new views, usually ultimately refreshed views; these new views didn't always include men in a possible future. Put yourself first for as long as it takes for you to see the world according to your own vision again. Minor irritations like being left by a man who doesn't appreciate you and certainly doesn't deserve you will only temporarily set you back.

If he left for another woman, resisting the temptation to blame 'the other woman' is strongly recommended. Women tend to try finding guilt and blame in the fellow female – *don't*. It's not her fault, even if she knew about you. Nobody, not even men, just leave overnight; the 'leaving' process usually starts long before its execution and typically in the head. The only blame anybody deserves is the leaving, unfaithful spouse. Providing 'the other woman' might have said 'no', yet another woman would have come along willing to say 'yes'. Whichever way one wants to turn it, he and only he is to blame.

Now that he has left – keep focused. Re-focus. Allow your brain to adjust, allow it all to settle in. You never know, perhaps this split is the best thing that could ever happen to you; it might not look or feel like it just yet but many of the women I have met would now confirm that life due to this experience has made them just that sexy extra bit stronger. If you have children to take care of, they more than anybody will appreciate this new strength of yours.

Despite it all, relationship – yes or no?
It's of course down to any individual as always, but 'yes' is the most often occurring emotion in many women when asked this question; however, many have already learnt it will only ever truly and satisfyingly work if one is willing to be rigorous enough to test-drive men until the one with the most positive overlapping qualities comes along. A relationship should never be based on biting one's tongue or strain one's neck in order to avoid conflict – if you find yourself doing this on a regular basis, re-think your relationship. Find the courage and bravery to change your life; if fighting for your independence is the only way out, so be it – fight. Easier said than done? No. Millions of women do it all the time; they break free from limiting compromises so often forced onto them when in a relationship. It's really quite simple – when breaking up seems the lesser of the stress than staying together, it's time to split.

No one in a relationship, not even men, should have to unhealthily adjust, change, pretend, get out of their skin or in any other way express a false inner self in order to accommodate the other half. Relationships built upon lies like these are not going to last and it will become a matter of who is going to announce the end first, him or you. Statistics show that seven out of ten splits are initiated by women; this is a number backed by the fact that it's usually women who are more willing to compromise at the beginning of a relationship. Hopes run high that whatever at the start of a liaison might not be ideal will perhaps change towards a more positive outcome in the future. To make matters worse, the wait turns into a habit. Women practically master the art of emotional endurance when it comes to giving men time to improve, an effort often ending in disappointment.

Quirks

The temptation to brand cute quirks as 'rubbish behaviour' and confuse them with irksome irritations is happening all the time. Once the level of irritation is hopelessly overstressed and tolerance is running out, even lovely little personal and usually entertaining 'areas of expertise' associated with one person turn coarse and are seen as everything but cute.

However, most oddities are not automatically limiting restrictions, although they are often perceived like that. The healthy middle ground is based on sensing the important difference between a cute quirk making a person special and an entire nuisance so often driving women crazy. In this case, a little healthy give and take has never done any harm, so bear with your man the next time he decides to stay in the toilet for hours or even longer in his shed or garage. The shed/garage for most men is their temple as much as Saks on Fifth Avenue in New York City is a haven for most women.

Separate bedrooms – separate lives?

Women's interest to solve the nightly snoring problem is unquenchable. I have worked with many who, when asked about 'beauty-sleep-time' could only grimace painfully. Men are often reacting towards this subject as if they have been caught committing a capital crime and mostly they don't understand how women can make such a big deal out of a little noise. But in women's eyes – and mainly ears – the endless hours spent deprived of sleep are similar to a capital crime. Tossing, turning, swearing, crying, ear plugs – nothing really works and finding some well-deserved rest becomes virtually impossible. The urge to strangle the man the bed is being shared with turns into an obsession.

Many ladies would love to sleep in a spare bedroom, providing there's one available. Men, however, often see this as a declaration of war – which, of course, it's not. Some women have told me that they sneak out during the night and return to the joint bedroom before the alarm goes off in the morning. It seems some men intuitively sense their women's attempts to escape in order to get some peace and sleep; just before they intend to leap out of the joint bed some arms appear from nowhere, wrapping themselves around the potential fugitive, and often women wonder whether it's curse or cure.

Don't despair – it's all about the right to choose, the right to express free will, the right to get some sleep – get your own bedroom with the bed of your choice. If no spare bedroom is available, the next best thing is a comfortable and proper sofa-bed and the unhappy female nocturnal creature one has turned into can eventually get some rest in the living room.

Talking to the male involved in this rebellion is the only way to attack the problem. If the relationship is how it should be – strong, built upon mutual understanding, love and care – it shouldn't be an issue. Both sides will greatly benefit from the freedom resulting from quality sleep. Personal preferences as far as sleep is concerned vary so much and so often, hardly ever are two people so compatible that sleep is what it should be – a rejuvenation.

To *not* disturb the co-sleeper is the overall idea. If one's man is objecting the natural quest for undisturbed sleep, whatever the reason might be (usually some insecure 'ego' reason), one should set the mobile phone alarm to 'vibrate' seven to ten times a night, just in case one gets some sleep, and wake the other half for educational explanation as many times. After a week he'll virtually be able to 'feel' the anguish one usually feels when woken seven to ten times a night and will agree to separate bedrooms. Don't just take my word for it, try it. Countless women have used this little trick successfully – and proper sleep has never felt better!

Separate beds are *not* a sign for 'the beginning of the end'. They are a mere symbol for a wonderfully mutual understanding of the fact that sleep is of most vital importance. Only insecure men have a problem with the whole 'two beds' issue. To teach them the significance of the matter at hand is highly recommended, as it will otherwise become both, dangerous for men (strangulation) and risky for women (suicidal tendencies stemming from lack of sleep, plus potentially murderous thoughts).

A little note on duvets

If sleeping in one bed is not representing a problem because one's lucky enough to live with a non-snorer, the general use of a double-duvet is the next in line of worries for many women I have met. Too heavy if super-king-size, too small if only a double-size, certainly too draughty in between the two sleepers – to just have one duvet of literally any shape or form is a nightmare for many. The solution to this annoying irritation couldn't be any easier – buy two single duvets and sleep in peace happily ever after. Some men believe a good old cuddle is not possible anymore once two covers have replaced the old habit of sharing one big one; in that case women can prove that, of course, hugging and more is still blissfully on the cards, if played right.

Leaving on the next train out

If one comes to the wise conclusion to end a relationship doomed to fail, thousands of years of humankind doing so have not yet revealed a way to avoid hurting the soon to be ex-partner. Unless one loathes the other, leaving will mostly hurt and mostly this pain is hated to be forced upon the partner. As there is unfortunately no other way, unless one sacrifices the own life based on feeling compassionate and even sorry for the other half, it usually helps trying to reason with the partner to be left. Outlining the major differences and the overall lack of proper compatibility often triggers a formerly not assumed to exist comprehension on the male's side – if one's lucky.

Men typically don't like my saying so, some even heavily object – when a man is left it's usually a

bleeding ego rather than the actual loss of the partner
he has to fight with (am resisting to use the word 'self-
pity'). Often underestimated, the male psyche might
be frail on the whole, especially when it comes to the
subject of 'sex', however, it is also miraculously quick
in repairing itself. Nature dictates to a man to hook
up again as soon as possible and convenient; bruised
souls and egos heal and the fun of relationship trouble
starts all over again. For everybody's sake, it is hoped
with great passion that a few points have been taken
in and even men's faith in finding the *fitting* partner
rather than just *any* partner has grown more objective
and certainly more appropriate.

Hopeless romantics? Enjoy!
Concentrating on finding not just the 'next', but
finding the fitting man remains appealing for most
women and they certainly should go ahead and
continue their search. Growing a thick skin and
working on the skills of dumping unsuitable men
easily is therefore strongly recommended, since
statistics have proven for the suitable man to show
his face to take some considerable amount of time.
Luckily, in spite of life being short, it should be long
enough to find that all important *one* match.

Women talk too much? No, men just don't talk enough!
The biggest trouble on the lack of compatibility-front
is women's ability to talk all day and all night, if need
be, and for men to rather not do so at all. Countless
books have been written about this subject alone, it's
that obvious a difference and so often criticised in
both directions and from both sides. Is there hope?

Quite frankly – no. This is probably the only 'big thing' both parties have to accept to never really fit – for women to talk and for men not to. However, it shouldn't stand in the way of pursuing to find the otherwise fitting relationship. If in doubt, pretend – for once for a good reason – to be quiet every now and then (ladies) or to be listening every now and then (gentlemen). Either way, it's often very amusing. The attempt to engage in a conversation by actually talking will be highly appreciated and men should be encouraged to try it from time to time. If no good for any other reason it's certainly going to be entertaining.

KISS – *Keep it short'n'simple*
If one decides to try talking over any issues evolving around the subject of one's relationship, one must remember the well known fact that men's attention span regarding any listening is not the most developed property in their DNA. Therefore it's strongly advised to keep anything to be discussed short and simple – after all we want to achieve a change for the better, or a quick end, not drive our men into depression facing their own limits, at least as far as communicational skills are concerned. A good sense of humour on any occasion also provides a great deal of support when handling men aiming for a good old chat.

Closing thoughts
For many women relationships and men are both, necessities and funny things. The idea to find the *one* fitting partner, the one a woman can entirely be herself with and feel the two beings create one unit, interlink and complement each other most wonderfully is so

appealing for many, the search might never end. Yet, it doesn't have to be a devastating experience either, even if things get wonky from time to time. As long as one is prepared to test-drive men and their abilities to 'fit' and doesn't shy away from facing the truth about life being best with as few as possible unhealthy compromises, the hunt for the appropriate Prince should continue passionately. Having a good portion of faith in the own abilities and qualities, an even bigger portion of humour and the biggest portion of self-confidence and self-acceptance possible, sooner or later, and certainly many women I have worked with, one will appreciate the vital fact of no one being neither 'wrong' nor 'right' to be the benchmark for a better relationship.

Whether one fits or one doesn't fit is a secret only two people at any one time can discover; preferably together.

'True power over your inner
self comes from within.
Once it's out, there's no stopping you.
Try it, but be warned, it's addictive.'

Ursula

The impact of self-acceptance

Filled with probably the most influential importance, this chapter represents the overall wrapping up of this little book of freedom. Self-confidence, self-acceptance, inner independence, immunity and untouchabilty – whatever word one has a special relationship with, without any of these powerful tools a woman's life is less successful, less content, less forward going and certainly less fun.

Some of us are born with all these attributes; nothing will ever shake some women while others find it hard to face the day, even without being surrounded by any specific or deeper troubles. The idea of this little book of freedom, however, is to hand out an ally for all those women who were not born as warriors. The correct attitude will help to even out any complicated challenges due to circumstances beyond any woman's control or influence; by accepting that an individual future is *also*, however, down to the individual perception, effort, focus, determination and, of course, that extra bit of luck will enable life to be seen as a little easier and clearer, too.

Self-acceptance is the most, absolutely most important and positively most influential and sincerely most powerful tool any woman can achieve within the female inner self. Nothing stronger is known beyond the magic of self-acceptance; not even witchcraft could do any better job. As the word in itself suggests, the acceptance of the *self* is the idea. Which sub-subject is chosen to tackle varies greatly from woman to woman. Having in common the bottom line that self-acceptance provides an almost not easily believable quality, all sub-subjects met with the armour of inner peace, calm, focus and therefore immunity are both, an eventually enlightening as well as charming aid to identify the inner strength.

Self-acceptance has also many faces; no matter which face shows itself, without it the *possible* will forever remain *impossible* as no one can ever be truly comfortable without the approval of the inner self. The unbelievably long trail of female underachievement in many women's individual lives proves this fact. Some might never escape the sticky side of life, and the constant and nerve-wracking journey towards gaining inner enlightenment often will see them remaining long-term travellers – I have met many women matching this profile.

Countless women feel the deep desire to be more self-confident; the thought that self-confidence automatically arises when whatever causes the lack of it is finally self-accepted seems to be a weird paradox. In other words, accept what you are fighting with and consider terminating this long haul fight. This will put both, you and your inner self at peace, will cause you to be less worried and will automatically make you come across as self-confident. Here are a few very popular and coincidentally the most realistic examples: –

Self-acceptance and smoking

If you're a smoker you have most likely tried to give up smoking every now and then or at least have thought about it. While 'tomorrow' so far has always seemed to be a better day to stop, my advice is don't stop, not today and not tomorrow. The more you try to fight what you don't really want to change the more at unease with yourself and the world you will be. Irritability and hatred of the world, the weather and the rest of it all will only ever result in you feeling even less of a good catch. To self-accept that you, for the time being, are a smoker is lots more attractive and shines with self-confidence; an endless festering over being too weak to stop and the constant battles only ever ending in losing against yourself does not suggest any positivity. Not worrying about any irritating judgement some criticising people come up with concerning your being a smoker will add extra confidence. Truly confident women who care less about what others might think have always and will always be lots more immune to outside views and criticism.

In shorter words, if you feel good, *you look good*.
As briefly mentioned in the introduction, as long as smoking feels better than quitting enjoy your smoke. To bore any smoker about the danger smoking

represents has already reached insulting proportions. Not being a smoker myself, however, understanding the aspects and feel-good factors linked to it I won't even go down this path and add to the slur.

Accept all possible and known consequences of smoking with pride – as long as you can practise self-acceptance none of the obvious side effects can force you into any influential self-doubts. The acceptance to be a smoker in the end is of such great relief to a person who has for years tried to fight the addiction, the overall positivity resulting from this will give you inner and outer smiles. Who cares whether they're wrinkly or not.

Self-acceptance and drinking

My father, so I was told, used to say 'The first and last drink never seems to agree with me; that why I usually pour them away'. What a wonderful wisdom.

As before with smoking, and somewhat providing that there are no real worrying medical implications, to self-accept that the enjoyment harvested from a drink or two or more is part of the personal freedom to be enjoyed in a far too short a life and is an overall and by far lots more attractive streak in a person that being stiff and stuck in uptight self-made and self-failed regulations. To self-accept that 'drink' is part of one's life is a crucial point that many non-drinking co-humans disagree with. All those who always try to communicate that they know better would reveal an anxious jealousy towards the self-confident, self-accepting 'drinker'. Perhaps the two opposite parties could over a glass or two discuss the meaning of it all.

Self-acceptance and ageing

The most important of all tools in a woman's existence
has never been needed more and has never been
more efficient than in the ageing mind. To self-accept
want can't be changed has given countless maturing
women I have worked with self-confidence beyond
my wildest dreams. In some cases I was under the
impression that facial wrinkles and hands covered
with age spots couldn't be waited for. How bizarre,
one should think. The message is as clear as the guilt-
free complexion of the ageing facial skin – life is worth
living, especially when feeling good about the inner
self. The outer self will always, *always* shine once
the inner self is content. Self-confidence can't but
dominate the appearance of a gorgeous, maturing
woman who has left the silly years of her youth finally
behind her. Every self-accepting maturing woman can
and will confirm this. Life has never been better;
getting older proves it daily and with every passing
second, some things *do* become better with age.

Self-acceptance and weight – overweight

The heavy subject that drives countless women to
breaking point is amongst the most important of all
subjects to concentrate and allocate self-acceptance
towards. As briefly mentioned in the chapter 'Diets'
earlier in the book, a woman twice the size she should
be, according to various health officials, but who's very
happy about her appearance, weight and attitude will
always appear to be one hundred times more attractive
than the woman half the size unhappy about being
unable to enjoy life due to misguided vanity and self-
prescribed starvation. The untouchability of being

happy within the own skin is so sensational, curvy celebrities demonstrate this to all womankind – and especially mankind. The entire 'size zero' discussion has one value only – money. The more the 'impossible' is being discussed and promises and information around the subject are being spread, the more money clever production teams of TV and other mass media channels make. To distant oneself from the absolutely ridiculous influences these calculating industries try to have is not just highly recommended – it shouldn't be dignified with any further attention.

Self-acceptance and weight – underweight
The skinny subject is apart from the overall dissimilarity of body weight in no shape or form different to the overweight subject – if one is in harmony with their underweight body, self-acceptance can be practised here as much as anywhere. Not every woman being too thin in the eyes of others is either sick or pretending to be ok. Some simply don't put on weight, especially not in the so-called 'right' places. To self-accept looking like the shadow of a thin tulip dancing in the wind is as much recommended as any other issue subjected to making a choice between being unhappy and festering or being happy and shining out a healthy immunity and untouchability. If 'big' isn't wrong, 'skinny' isn't wrong, either.

Self-acceptance and being single
One doesn't have to be exposed to the world like Rachel has been in the chapter 'Single' earlier in the book to understand why some women prefer the

lifestyle of being single – forever. Behind a screen like sometimes shown on TV, unrecognisable to the watching world, many spoken for women I have interviewed were actually surprisingly jealous of their fellow women's' spinster status. To self-accept that being single is, in fact, a great privilege and not just plain bad luck seems at times forgotten though. To enjoy this chosen way of life with all its freedom is perhaps appealing to many, yet at the same time it's often the cause for self-doubts and concerns. A nagging mother requesting grandchildren is one of those characters who every now and then drives single ladies up the wall with questions about the justification and the feasibility of being alone by choice. Don't despair. Practising self-acceptance is here as much as anywhere the best method to gain wonderful freedom, untouchability and inner immunity. Being a woman of substance complete in oneself carries qualities many can't but be envious of – even the own mothers.

Self-acceptance against the rest of the world
Don't be too hard on yourself and don't allow others to be either. You are what and who you are and should be proud to be such an individual. Many women I have met who were fighting with self-confidence issues had to face the outside claim from so-called caring others to know better, constantly criticising the own decisions and choices. With so much external pressure it's no wonder one would consider going insane a healthier option than practising self-acceptance and fighting for it.

I've heard and seen it so many times – perfectly healthy smokers who might perhaps enjoy ten or so cigarettes a day are being treated by some people as if their death is imminent. Women with one stone or so too much on the hips and keeping this weight are being treated as if any moment they will die from obesity. Completely happy single ladies are being treated as if on loneliness-death row or worse – they have to go on blind dates arranged by friends and family. Skinny women are force-fed against their will. The woman enjoying a drink on a regular basis can't but be an alcoholic – so it's assumed with great unfairness. This list could be very long, so I better stop right here.

It's time the downsized ego gets the replenishment treatment. Free yourself from this nonsense – your being fine with how things are is all that matters. And if not, it's up to you when and how to attack any change you might desire. If at any one time you decide you need help, you'll know where to head; our world is full of advice leaflets, every corner of life holds a leaflet for any imaginable problem, ready to be picked up.

The best of all possible allies
The real impact of self-acceptance and self-confidence results in untouchable freedom. The irresistible attraction one glows with while literally bathing in a previously unknown inner peace gives women powers and attention beyond anybody's first assumptions. Whatever situation, virtually any circumstance can be met with such re-assured central strength that one often asks why any of these obvious features have not been discovered any earlier in life.

Summery

Self-acceptance is the most important feature in a woman's world; after having mastered the art of practising self-acceptance one can be an overweight, smoking, drinking, middle-aged, wrinkly, rebellious single woman who eventually will have all her courage together to tell her mother that she's an independent lesbian who hates her mother's sight. Highly unorthodox? Perhaps. Liberating? Beyond belief.

In other words, nobody needs to accept you but you. Smoker, drinker, overweight, underweight, single, disabled, divorced and whatever else, these are all factors one might think influence the true inner self. Once absurd outside manipulations and authorities are controlled the harm they can cause to the inner side of life is limited and in an ideal world even completely banned.

Self-acceptance is not about giving in or giving up due to weakness; quite the opposite is the case. Self-acceptance requires a good bunch of inner strength. Anybody self-accepting will always feel and will always be seen as a strong personality.

Once this fact is undeniably established, there's truly no stopping you.

Conclusion

What a journey! Congratulations, you've come a long way. Reading this little book of freedom, whichever subject or subjects you were enquiring about, was the first big step into a new awareness.

Learning that others out there find themselves in comparable situations, face similar challenges and suffer parallel consequences I have found to uplift many women beyond their initial comprehensions.

Facing the reality of old enemies at times being persistent but conquerable should eliminate any woman's fear of the tomorrow with a healthy appetite and curiosity to explore unknown territory. Every inch further mapped on the atlas called 'life' will convert known troubles into unknown pleasures – a truly relieving experience, cherished by many.

Breaking free from being a nonsensical man's sweet little affair; establishing or rediscovering love-making from a new perspective; ditching useless diets everlastingly; evaluating one's relationship and the inevitably connected man; discovering the partner's ex's similar status and familiar position; climbing a mountain, escaping childhood influences; exorcising worries of unavoidable ageing; releasing one's soul from overbearing family ties; finding solace in being single and the overdue liberation from the homemade comfort zone – the complexity of the emotional cages and unhealthy compromises crushed by these achievements represent an almost overpowering might.

Any possible good outcome will be felt for the rest of one's life. The relief achieved, paired with a healthy curiosity to take the years to come even further, will work wonders on self-confidence, inner independence, untouchability, immunity and self-acceptance.

I wish you well on your remarkable, further journey. At any one time you might find irritating obstacles thrown into your way, trust that you're armed – for barriers to be handled competently even when facing a little fight here or there is a wonderful side effect of having come this far.

An ancient far eastern mantra, regardless of any personal choice of faith or even atheism, is celebrated gratefully; as most good guidance, it's brief – *God made me a woman; I am a woman to be. Now, now, now.*

Women the world over find great solace and solidarity in this truly amazing wisdom without jeopardising any rewarded independence. Once employed, the mind practises freedom and sovereignty on a *bonus* level, and with life being too short for cheap cling film, it's time to live it.

All the best,

Maren Peters

Lightning Source UK Ltd.
Milton Keynes UK

176598UK00001B/45/P